SCRIPTURAL RO
COMMERCE

BOOK 6

THE ECONOMY
OF GOD

TOM PETERSEN

WITH

JIM PETERSEN
DONALD MCGILCHRIST
JERRY WHITE
GLENN MCMAHAN, EDITOR

THIRD EDITION

CONTENTS

FOREWORD

To link the words "Scriptural" and "Commerce" in the title of a book series may seem odd to today's popular mindset. Even in Christian circles, many people assume that the Scriptures have little to say about business, innovation, or daily work. This assumption, unfortunately, is based on a long history of misguided thinking that divided our lives into "secular" and "sacred" compartments. This fragmentation has its consequences. Separating theology from the workplace has frustrated many working men and women, leaving them to feel that their professional lives have no significance in relation to God's purposes in the world.

Having experienced this frustration first-hand, a group of theologians and businessmen set out in the mid-1990s to research what the Scriptures teach about work and commerce. Over the course of six years, they discovered what author Paul Minear stated so well: "The Bible is a book by workers, about workers, for workers." Inspired by what they learned, the original team published the *Scriptural Roots of Commerce*. What you are reading now is the third version of the "SRC," as it's commonly known.

What is commerce? In our view, commerce includes the broad scope of all economic activity at every level. This definition involves all professions—medicine, teaching, science, construction, military, mining, law. Commerce covers a vast array of interactions. It is highly relational. It plays a significant role in forming the culture in which we live. In fact, very little happens in life without commerce.

God gives us the freedom and responsibility to shape our world (for better or worse). So, as we engage in commerce, our decisions and actions matter not just for our own lives, but also for our communities and even the next generation. This sobering responsibility should compel us to rethink the status quo and to pay close attention to what God desires for work and commerce. After all, he reveals his designs for life not to constrain us but to help us thrive. The Scriptures reveal a God who cares about commerce because he cares about people.

The *Scriptural Roots of Commerce* provides a practical and accessible framework to help you explore work and commerce through the lens of the Scriptures. The books will not give you canned answers that force you toward predetermined outcomes, but will help you explore and think about what the Scriptures reveal about your professional life.

Obviously, these books require your time and commitment. We believe this is one of the best attributes of the series! In our hurried and impatient world, we are tempted to skim across an ocean of superficial information, filling our heads with unrelated facts and applying very little of what we learn. Our attention spans wane under an onslaught of unrelated sound-bites, tweets, and ads. The cacophony presents us with no purposeful, over-arching story. Not surprisingly, we long for meaning. By contrast, the SRC will help you build your worldview and grow as a person. It encourages us to slow down, think deeply, and live innovatively alongside a committed group of close friends.

Our hope is expressed in our mission statement: "to help men and women align their lives with biblical truth, so that they can survive and flourish in the workplace and spread purpose and hope within their contexts."

Glenn McMahan
Chairman
Global Commerce Network

GETTING THE MOST OUT OF THIS STUDY

The Scriptural Roots of Commerce offers a sequence for developing your thinking about the most critical matters of human life. Book 1 takes us toward a deeper understanding of God, the foundation for everything else. Book 2 helps us better comprehend human nature and what that means for the way we live and work. Book 3 presents the kingdom of God within which our lives find meaning and hope. The fourth book unveils the crucial role of relationships in commerce, and God's design for our relationships. Book 5 presents a theology of work that helps us understand why work is meaningful. The last book in the series offers a much needed biblical understanding of wealth and finances.

We recommend that you work through the books according to the sequence described above. However, depending on your interests and needs, the books can be used out of order.

Importantly, the SRC is designed to be studied with peers. We learn and grow best in iron-sharpens-iron friendships. Participants often provide excellent (and free) life coaching and business consulting for one another.

Although the SRC stimulates serious thinking, it is not only an intellectual exercise. What we learn should be lived, and what we live helps us learn. We encourage you to think creatively about how to apply what you learn from the Scriptures in your workplace and community.

Forming an SRC group is simple. It only takes someone to make the invitations, set a time and place, and create an environment where people feel free to bring questions and insights. The SRC provides the content and the basic structure. Because the SRC is about discovery, facilitators don't need to have all the answers. If you would like to start a group, Global Commerce Network has published a Facilitator's Guide to help.

Many people ask how long it takes to go through the series. What's the hurry? Some groups study a section at home before meeting together. Others prefer to read and discuss small sections for the first time during each meeting. The important thing is to take your time, think deeply, live what you learn, and enjoy the friendships.

If you need help, write us at: info@globalcommercenetwork.com.

Overview of The SRC

The subject matter in these six books is broad enough to shape not only the way we work, but also our approach to every sphere of life. The first three books focus on aligning our worldview with the truth of the Gospel. The last three books help us apply this understanding in our relationships, work, and economy.

Book 1: Why God Matters

What we believe about God affects everything, including our work. This book unveils God's nature, giving us an opportunity to explore his creativity, entrepreneurial spirit, justice, love, and forgiveness. A growing relationship with God will have a dramatic impact on our professional and personal lives.

Book 2: Why People Matter

All work and commerce is an expression of human nature. People are capable of amazing goodness, but we struggle with deep undercurrents of selfishness, greed, envy, and even hatred. If we don't have a realistic understanding of human nature, it will be difficult to make sense of our lives or the workplace. A true view of who we are will improve our ability to renew the workplace so that people and businesses thrive.

Book 3: Life in the Kingdom

The kingdom of God is the big picture. It is the stage upon which God and people interact. It's the arena in which God fulfills his purposes. We need to understand God's kingdom and his purposes to have a true perspective about the world around us and how we are to live. God calls us to live and work as citizens of his kingdom even though it often exists in tension with our culture.

Book 4: Working Together

All commerce is relational. We relate to clients, suppliers, colleagues, bosses, and employees. Surprisingly, most companies never give the relational element of commerce much thought. But if we can relate well in the workplace (and at home) by growing in character traits such as humility, integrity, and forgiveness, our lives and work will flourish.

Book 5: The Meaning of Work

We spend most of our lives working. Do our jobs mean anything to God? The Meaning of Work offers a positive answer to that question. Early in the story, we discover a God who works and who has designed us to work. We explore the truth that all work done in faith is sacred and purposeful. The study then helps us discover how our professional lives can be integrated with God's restoration of a broken world. It closes with an investigation of physical and spiritual rest in the context of our stressful times.

Book 6: The Economy of God

In this study, we explore a biblical perspective of material and spiritual wealth. God's material world provides a capital base that we can use for the glory of God by working it and caring for it. In God's economy, even those who are materially poor can be spiritually rich, and those who are materially wealthy might find they are spiritually poor.

The Importance of Your Worldview

This study, without imposing a dogma, helps you understand and rethink your worldview in light of the Scriptures. So, it might be helpful to understand how your deepest beliefs affect your life.

Worldview: A worldview is a composite of beliefs, usually adopted from one's culture, media, traditions, family, education, and religion. Every person has a worldview, even if it has been formed in an *ad hoc* manner. It shapes the way we see and interpret reality, the way we answer the big questions of life: How do I understand the world and its origins? Who am I? What makes life meaningful? What is my belief about God? What happens after death?

Values: Our worldview influences our values. A value is something so important to us that it motivates our actions and decisions. If, for example, I believe there is no life after death, that belief will influence what I find to be most important. Living for the moment, a *carpe diem* approach to life, would probably be my ambition.

Behavior: In this way, our worldview and values shape our behavior and choices. If self-fulfillment is our primary driving value, our behavior will follow. We will spend a lot of time and energy pursuing things that we hope will satisfy that desire. So, our choices and actions each day reflect something about what we really believe.

These three factors serve as a basic framework for understanding ourselves and our society. They also instruct us in how to grow and change. Trying to change just our behavior without addressing our beliefs will usually fail because nothing has changed in our minds and hearts!

Worldview is not just a matter of the intellect. The Bible says: "Above all else, guard your heart, for it is the wellspring of life" (Proverbs 4:23). So, what you believe about God is influenced by your will and heart. The Scriptures make it clear that if a person's heart is bent on maintaining independence from God, all the best arguments in favor of God won't change anything. The intellect is crucial, but there must also be humility in the heart.

The SRC begins by expanding our understanding of God in order to align our lives with him, the sole source of life. As we do this, every area of our lives will be enriched. How do you answer the big questions?

WHAT IS THE BIBLE?

The Bible is without a doubt the most influential book in all of history. Basing their lives on the Bible, men and women have established constitutional governments, opposed totalitarian regimes, ended slavery, developed science, founded universities, worked to cure sickness, served the poor, fought against racism, and humanized commerce. Most importantly, the Bible has been the cornerstone for establishing the infinite and unconditional worth of every human being.

The Bible is a collection of books, a library, written over a period of 1,600 years from approximately B.C. 1500 to A.D. 100. Its contents are inextricably rooted in history. The Bible accurately presents specific and testable details about kings, construction, battles, cities, and currencies.

The books of the Bible also portray the full spectrum of human nature. In prose and poetry, the authors express their deepest longings and questions. Others publicly confess their worst behavior and attitudes. King David's adultery, Peter's denial of Christ, Paul's violence against the early church—it's all there for us to read. Clearly, the Bible was not written by public relations specialists trying to put a positive spin on religious ideas. Instead, the Bible is authentic and honest, addressing the complexities and questions faced by every person.

About forty different authors contributed to the Bible. The writers include farmers, soldiers, prophets, kings, musicians, statesmen, fishermen, doctors, and apostles. Given the diversity of the authors and the time-span of the writings, one would expect to find an unintelligible hodgepodge of conflicting ideas. To the contrary, there is amazing congruence, with each part contributing to a single, central story. This story is about a just and holy God taking every initiative to show us who he is, what he's like, and how we can live whole and meaningful lives. His motive? He loves us!

The Old Testament provides the history of God's involvement with the nations, primarily with the Israelites. God gradually reveals his holiness, justice, and love. He communicates through the beauty and order of the physical universe, through his messengers (who often wound up murdered), and through his tangible action in history. Many chapters foretell the coming of Jesus, some in great detail. By the time Jesus arrived, most Jewish people knew exactly how to recognize him when they saw him.

The New Testament begins with four accounts of Jesus' life, each from a slightly different perspective. These books are called the Gospels. Then, in the book of Acts, there is a detailed account of the birth of the young churches that sprang up across the Roman Empire in the first century. The remainder of the New Testament consists of personal letters that helped the early faith communities to thrive as followers of Christ.

One of those letters, written by Peter, explains why the Scriptures are so extraordinary: "Above all, you must understand that no prophecy of Scripture came about by the prophet's own interpretation. For prophecy never had its origin in the will of man, but men spoke from God as they were carried along by the Holy Spirit."

Because the Bible is thus inspired, it gives us God's wisdom for living a meaningful and joyful life. It addresses issues such as relationships, emotional health, child rearing, work, business, finances, leadership, and government. As you become familiar with the Bible and benefit from its matchless wisdom, you will understand the importance of Peter's words.

May you be inspired to build, innovate, and serve as you interact with the Bible.

THE ECONOMY OF GOD
INTRODUCTION

Most of us have probably never considered the idea that there is an economy within God's kingdom. When most people think of an economy they usually imagine gross national product, stock markets, unemployment rates and investment banks. Indeed, an economy is the broad, interdependent system within which a society functions.

There is an economy within God's kingdom and it's ultimately about people. The engine that drives this economy is God's relentless love for people who, in becoming a part of his kingdom, are enabled to thrive and flourish according to their design. This is the only economy that never suffers a loss. It is eternal, unshakeable.

The economy of God operates on different principles and values than the world's economies. Learning about these values stirs us to rethink popular ideas of wealth and economics. In God's economy, those who are materially poor can find they are spiritually rich, and those who are materially rich might discover their spiritual poverty. In the economy of God, the least can become the greatest. Justice and freedom are grounded in God's nature, not in subjective human whims.

God's economy profoundly alters the significance of our work and commerce, even when that labor seems mundane. Our work, our buying and selling, our production of goods and services, our investing or our teaching—all of it can serve to fuel this eternal economy. Our labors can nurture the expansion of God's kingdom through the relationships that are inherent to our work. God notices our service, and it matters to him.

As participants in the economy of God, we are faced with constant tensions as we work and live within human economies. On the global level, the issues of wealth and poverty are of primary concern. In many countries endemic corruption and other greed-driven injustices foster violence and cripple economies, thus robbing its citizens.

We also experience tensions on the personal level. Of what value, you might ask, is my investment portfolio in the eternal scheme of things? What about my business? What am I supposed to do with it? Does it mean anything at all? Or, I am working two jobs and barely getting by, and God tells me not to worry! Is he kidding?

In the first section of this study, *The Economy of God,* we will examine what the Bible reveals about the nature of his economy and our place in the context of his economic purposes. This will lead us to examine the things God most values, and it will become obvious how different God's economy is from the world's. Having this understanding is crucial if we are to effectively work with God in restoring the broken economies in which we live.

The second section, "Capital," provides a biblical understanding of a very misunderstood economic foundation. The Scriptures identify several types of capital, and they all come from God. Capital gives us the basis for growth and fruitfulness, both in material and spiritual terms. Capital is the basic component for economic survival in any society.

Section three, "Poverty and Wealth," brings these broad concepts into the context of family and community—into our daily work and relationships. Economics and commerce are not just about a nation's Gross Domestic Product. God's economy takes place in the context of community and family. These are the contexts in which we make our financial decisions, support our children, and contribute to our society.

Section four is titled "Economies in Conflict." To choose to live according to God's economy will necessarily bring us into tension with the world's economies. So how do we aim to follow God's principles while trying to survive in a corrupt world? The Scriptures give us wisdom and guidance. Without a transformation of our hearts in relation to our resources, we can never experience the freedom God intended for us.

In section five, "Living Generously," we will examine how to integrate our lives by imitating God and his generous nature. The Scriptures tell us that he sacrifices so that we might flourish. The deeply generous nature of God is our model for a new way of living, one that is not about self, but about others. This implies a personal cost. But, paradoxically, this way of generous living is the key to experiencing meaning and joy. As Jesus said, "Whoever loses his life for my sake will find it (Matthew 10:39)."

Ultimately, wealth and economics in God's economy is about people. Max Lucado says this: "When you are in the final days of your life, what will you want? Will you hug that college degree in the walnut frame? Will you ask to be carried to the garage so that you can sit in your car? Will you find comfort in re-reading your financial statement? Of course not. What will matter then will be people. If relationships will matter most then, shouldn't they matter most now"?

Even the roots of our word "economy" extend from a highly relational idea expressed in the ancient Greek language. As described in book 4, a word for economy is *oikonomia.* This term also described the household, meaning an entire relational network of parents, grandparents, children, servants, workers. Earning money, worshiping God, work, and relation-ships were integrated. Everything was relational. We see this in many New Testament writings.

The term oikonomia also implies the active administration of wealth and family and God's purposes. This would include raising children and producing wealth, as the following scriptures demonstrate.

". . . this grace was given me: to preach to the Gentiles the unsearchable riches of Christ, and to make plain to everyone the administration *(oikono-mia)* of this mystery, which for ages past was kept hidden in God, who created all things" (Ephesians 3:8-9).

"He made known to us the mystery of his will according to his good pleasure, which he purposed in Christ, to be put into effect *(oikonomia)* when the times will have reached their fulfillment" (Ephesians 1:9-10).

Crucial to all of this is that the Scriptures provide a framework for integrating our professional and financial lives with the purposes and designs of God. The more we can understand and live within these designs, the more our lives will gain meaning, and the more we will flourish.

SECTION 1
THE ECONOMY OF GOD

God's creative action began with his heart of love. He decided to provide a breathtaking gift—his creation. It is a gift so vast, so spectacular, that it would not be surpassed until the gift of the Messiah, his Son.

To properly understand economics, commerce, and the management of our resources, we must first understand this beginning—the first economic transaction.

The materialist philosophy of the past 250 years has drastically changed the founding principles and values that undergird modern economics. As Adam Smith recognized, God was being replaced in economics by an "invisible hand," and the economic motivation of love for neighbor was being replaced by "self-interest." The Industrial Revolution treated people as mere "employees" required to work in a giant shed with a smoke stack. Production within the economy has since become mechanistic, increasingly analyzed, managed, and reduced to abstraction. All that seems to remain are amoral concepts of supply and demand. And, not surprisingly, the results often dissatisfy us. We feel uneasy. We wonder if it's meaningful. We fear. But we have been so infected by this stark, cold materialism that even when we sense the inhumanity and godlessness of it, we shrug and say to ourselves, "This is business."

As we will see in this section, God's economy upends the intellectual assumptions and popular trends of our age. The economy of God is radically different, primarily because *people* are the ultimate purpose of all his economic activity. People are not meant to be cogs in an impersonal system of production.

The first two chapters of Genesis provide the most significant description of God's construction of the material world. Over the course of creation described in Genesis, God is meticulously preparing the physical conditions needed for human life. The scope of his material creation is breathtaking, precisely fine-tuned and ordered, and amazingly beautiful. Finally, he created a spiritual and material being called "human."

1. As you read the following Scriptures, attempt to discover God's primary motivations for creating the material world. Why did he, after all, create our material universe and then create us?

GENESIS 1:26-31

Then God said, "Let us make mankind in our image, in our likeness, so that they may rule over the fish in the sea and the birds in the sky, over the livestock and all the wild animals, and over all the creatures that move along the ground." So God created mankind in his own image, in the image of God he created them; male and female he created them. God blessed them and said to them, "Be fruitful and increase in number; fill the earth and subdue it. Rule over the fish in the sea and the birds in the sky and over every living creature that moves on the ground." Then God said, "I give you every seed-bearing plant on the face of the whole earth and every tree that has fruit with seed in it. They will be yours for food. And to all the beasts of the earth and all the birds in the sky and all the creatures that move along the ground—everything that has the breath of life in it—I give every green plant for food." And it was so. God saw all that he had made, and it was very good. And there was evening, and there was morning—the sixth day.

> All the seemingly arbitrary and unrelated constants in physics have one strange thing in common—these are precisely the values you need if you want to have a universe capable of producing life. . . . the universe had apparently been directed toward one goal: the creation of human life.
> *Patrick Glynn*

GENESIS 2:5-9

Now no shrub had yet appeared on the earth and no plant had yet sprung up, for the Lord God had not sent rain on the earth and there was no one to work the ground, but streams came up from the earth and watered the whole surface of the ground. Then the Lord God formed a man from the dust of the ground and breathed into his nostrils the breath of life, and the man became a living being. Now the Lord God had planted a garden in the east, in Eden; and there he put the man he had formed. The Lord God made all kinds of trees grow out of the ground— trees that were pleasing to the eye and good for food.

> The more I examine the universe and study the details of its architecture, the more I find that the universe in some sense knew we were coming.
> *Physicist Freeman Dyson*

DEUTERONOMY 32:8-9

When the Most High gave the nations their inheritance, when he divided all mankind, he set up boundaries for the peoples according to the number of the sons of Israel. For the Lord's portion is his people . . .

PSALM 97:6
The heavens proclaim his righteousness, and all peoples see his glory.

> The laws and constants of the universe are finely tuned to allow life. So, too, are the physical and chemical properties of elements such as carbon and simple compounds such as water. So, too, is earth's location in the galaxy and solar system. So, too, are details of the earth's size, composition, and history. So, too, as the geneticist Michael Denton has forcefully argued, . . . are the more complex categories of the molecules of life.
> *Biochemist Michael Behe*

ACTS 14:17
Yet he has not left himself without testimony: He has shown kindness by giving you rain from heaven and crops in their seasons; he provides you with plenty of food and fills your hearts with joy.

ROMANS 1:20
For since the creation of the world God's invisible qualities—his eternal power and divine nature—have been clearly seen, being understood from what has been made, so that people are without excuse.

> The first thing the word home brings to mind is a place, then the next and perhaps most crucial thing is people and maybe ultimately a single person.
> *Frederick Buechner*

EPHESIANS 1:3-14
Praise be to the God and Father of our Lord Jesus Christ, who has blessed us in the heavenly realms with every spiritual blessing in Christ. For he chose us in him before the creation of the world to be holy and blameless in his sight. In love he predestined us for adoption to sonship through Jesus Christ, in accordance with his pleasure and will— to the praise of his glorious grace, which he has freely given us in the One he loves. In him we have redemption through his blood, the forgiveness of sins, in accordance with the riches of God's grace that he lavished on us. With all wisdom and understanding, he made known to us the mystery of his will according to his good pleasure, which he purposed in Christ, to be put into effect when the times reach their fulfillment—to bring unity to all things in heaven and on earth under Christ. In him we were also chosen, having been predestined according to the plan of him who works out everything in conformity with the purpose of his will, in order that we, who were the first to put our hope in Christ, might be for the praise of his glory. And you also were included in Christ when you heard the message of truth, the gospel of your salvation. When you believed, you were marked in him with a seal, the promised Holy Spirit, who is a deposit guaranteeing our inheritance until the redemption of those who are God's possession—to the praise of his glory.

1.1 Notice that God did not just create the material world; he specifically created a home for human beings. What impresses you about the "home" God created? What does this tell you about God's relational nature? About us?

1.2 The beauty and function of the material world have spiritual significance. They tell of the existence and glory of God. What attribute of God do you observe in creation that stirs in you a desire to worship? How is this an antidote for materialism?

1.3 What do you think most motivated God, who demonstrated remarkable entrepreneurial zeal, to create the universe?

1.4 Identify two or three aspects of God's creative work that most stand out to you.

1.5 What can we learn from these passages about the nature of God's economy?

∽

God's economy places people as the highest value. People--regardless of their mental or physical abilities, regardless of their age or race--have infinite worth in God's value system. Only from that foundation can any economic activity find its meaning. In God's economy, people are not seen as the means to some other end; they are the focus of God's economic purposes. In fact, the Greek word for "economy" is *oikonomia,* which is a derivative of the Greek word for household. It is a family, a people interconnected by service to one another. This is what God's economy is about. He is creating his household, adopting children into his family. His relational nature is revealed in his economy.

2. What links can you discover about God's relational character and his economic motivations and designs?

JOHN 17:6-8
I have revealed you to those whom you gave me out of the world. They were yours; you gave them to me and they have obeyed your word. Now they know that everything you have given me comes from you. For I gave them the words you gave me and they accepted them. They knew with certainty that I came from you, and they believed that you sent me.

> . . . the Bible has been the greatest humanizing force in history. It drove the movement for the abolition of slavery and prompted care for the weak, such as widows, orphans, the handicapped, and leprosy patients. From liberating and rehabilitating temple prostitutes to reforming prisons and bringing sanity and morality to wars, the biblical tradition has been the most powerful civilizing force. *Vishal Mangalwadi*

JOHN 17:16-23
They are not of the world, even as I am not of it. Sanctify them by the truth; your word is truth. As you sent me into the world, I have sent them into the world. For them I sanctify myself, that they too may be truly sanctified. "My prayer is not for them alone. I pray also for those who will believe in me through their message, that all of them may be one, Father, just as you are in me and I am in you. May they also be in us so that the world may believe that you have sent me. I have given them the glory that you gave me, that they may be one as we are one—I in them and you in me—so that they may be brought to complete unity. Then the world will know that you sent me and have loved them even as you have loved me.

> In the context of the brutal and impersonal Roman Empire, ". . . Christianity taught that mercy is one of the primary virtues—that a merciful God requires humans to be merciful. Moreover, the corollary that because God loves humanity, Christians may not please God unless they love one another was something entirely new." *Rodney Stark*

HEBREWS 2:10-13
In bringing many sons and daughters to glory, it was fitting that God, for whom and through whom everything exists, should make the pioneer of their salvation perfect through what he suffered. Both the one who makes people holy and those who are made holy are of the same family. So Jesus is not ashamed to call them brothers and sisters. He says, "I will declare your name to my brothers and sisters; in the assembly I will sing your praises." And again, "I will put my trust in him." And again he says, "Here am I, and the children God has given me."

1 JOHN 3:1-3
See what great love the Father has lavished on us, that we should be called children of God! And that is what we are! The reason the world does not know us is

that it did not know him. Dear friends, now we are children of God, and what we will be has not yet been made known. But we know that when Christ appears, we shall be like him, for we shall see him as he is. All who have this hope in him purify themselves, just as he is pure.

> Christianity [in the first century] did not grow because of miracle working in the marketplaces, . . . or because Constantine said it should, or even because the martyrs gave it such credibility. It grew because Christians constituted an intense community. . . . *Rodney Stark*

ROMANS 8:23

Not only so, but we ourselves, who have the first fruits of the Spirit, groan inwardly as we wait eagerly for our adoption to sonship . . .

2.1. Why is God so committed to building a relationship with us?

2.2 How might these truths impact the way you think about your work and profession?

꙳

It's clear that God's heart is fully set on drawing a family of people to himself for an eternal relationship, one that starts here and now. He's calling us to himself and to a life of community with one another. As we humble ourselves and surrender to the authority of Jesus, we become part of an eternal kingdom that transcends all the world's politics and economies.

3. Scriptures, such as John 3:16 and John 17 have shown us that God's economy is ultimately about his relationship with people. For this relationship to occur, however, it cost God the life of his Son.

1 PETER 1:18-19

For you know that it was not with perishable things such as silver or gold that you were redeemed from the empty way of life handed down to you from your ancestors, but with the precious blood of Christ, a lamb without blemish or defect.

1 JOHN 2:2

He is the atoning sacrifice for our sins, and not only for ours but also for the sins of the whole world.

ROMANS 5:1-11

Therefore, since we have been justified through faith, we have peace with God through our Lord Jesus Christ, through whom we have gained access by faith into this grace in which we now stand. And we boast in the hope of the glory of God. Not only so, but we also glory in our sufferings, because we know that suffering produces perseverance; perseverance, character; and character, hope. And hope does not put us to shame, because God's love has been poured out into our hearts through the Holy Spirit, who has been given to us. You see, at just the right time, when we were still powerless, Christ died for the ungodly. Very rarely will anyone die for a righteous person, though for a good person someone might possibly dare to die. But God demonstrates his own love for us in this: While we were still sinners, Christ died for us. Since we have now been justified by his blood, how much more shall we be saved from God's wrath through him! For if, while we were God's enemies, we were reconciled to him through the death of his Son, how much more, having been reconciled, shall we be saved through his life! Not only is this so, but we also boast in God through our Lord Jesus Christ, through whom we have now received reconciliation.

> If God was prepared to let us off (forgive us), why on earth did he not do so? And what possible point could there be in punishing an innocent person (Jesus) instead? None at all that I can see, if you are thinking of punishment in the police-court sense. On the other hand, if you think of a debt, there is plenty of point in a person who has some assets paying it on behalf of someone who has not. . . . When one person has got himself into a hole, the trouble of getting him out usually falls on a kind friend. *C.S. Lewis*

ROMANS 3:24-26

. . . all are justified freely by his grace through the redemption that came by Christ Jesus. God presented Christ as a sacrifice of atonement, through the shedding of his blood, to be received by faith. He did this to demonstrate his righteousness, because in his forbearance he had left the sins committed beforehand unpunished—he did it to demonstrate his righteousness at the present time, so as to be just and the one who justifies those who have faith in Jesus.

3.1 Why do you think our relationship with God required such a costly sacrifice?

3.2 God is holy and we are unholy. How could a God of justice restore a relationship with us so as to include us in his family?

4. The sacrifice of Jesus was the ultimate demonstration of God's love. Throughout the Scriptures we see that sacrifice is an inherent aspect of God's nature, and therefore his economy. The sacrificial nature of God's economy sets it apart from the world's economies. What counter-cultural aspects of his economy do you see emerging in these passages?

ROMANS 12:1-2

Therefore, I urge you, brothers and sisters, in view of God's mercy, to offer your bodies as a living sacrifice, holy and pleasing to God—this is your true and proper worship. Do not conform to the pattern of this world, but be transformed by the renewing of your mind. Then you will be able to test and approve what God's will is—his good, pleasing and perfect will.

LUKE 14:12-14

Then Jesus said to his host, "When you give a luncheon or dinner, do not invite your friends, your brothers or sisters, your relatives, or your rich neighbors; if you do, they may invite you back and so you will be repaid. But when you give a banquet, invite the poor, the crippled, the lame, the blind, and you will be blessed. Although they cannot repay you, you will be repaid at the resurrection of the righteous."

1 CORINTHIANS 13:3-6

If I give all I possess to the poor and give over my body to hardship that I may boast, but do not have love, I gain nothing. Love is patient, love is kind. It does not envy, it does not boast, it is not proud. It does not dishonor others, it is not self-seeking, it is not easily angered, it keeps no record of wrongs. Love does not delight in evil but rejoices with the truth.

1 CORINTHIANS 15:58

Therefore, my dear brothers and sisters, stand firm. Let nothing move you. Always give yourselves fully to the work of the Lord, because you know that your labor in the Lord is not in vain.

> Jesus' heroism replaced brutality with love, pride with meekness, and domination over others with self-sacrificing service. He exemplified this when he humbled himself, took a basin of water and a servant's towel, and started washing his disciples' feet. This, he said, is what the kingdom of God is all about. *Vishal Mangalwadi*

PHILIPPIANS 2:5-8

In your relationships with one another, have the same mindset as Christ Jesus: Who, being in very nature God, did not consider equality with God something to be used to his own advantage; rather, he made himself nothing by taking the very nature of a servant, being made in human likeness. And being found in appearance as a man, he humbled himself by becoming obedient to death—even death on a cross!

Through the half-open door in one room of the huts I saw Pastor Bonhoeffer, before taking off his prison garb, kneeling on the floor praying fervently to his God. . . . At the place of execution, he again said a short prayer and then climbed the steps to the gallows, brave and composed. His death ensued after a few seconds. In the almost fifty years that I worked as a doctor, I have hardly ever seen a man die so entirely submissive to the will of God.
A concentration camp doctor, about Dietrich Bonhoeffer's execution by Nazis

JOHN 12:23-26
Jesus replied, "The hour has come for the Son of Man to be glorified. Very truly I tell you, unless a kernel of wheat falls to the ground and dies, it remains only a single seed. But if it dies, it produces many seeds. Anyone who loves their life will lose it, while anyone who hates their life in this world will keep it for eternal life. Whoever serves me must follow me; and where I am, my servant also will be. My Father will honor the one who serves me."

Most of our brother Christians showed unbounded love and loyalty, never sparing themselves and thinking only of one another. Heedless of danger, they took charge of the sick, attending to their every need and ministering to them in Christ, and with them departed this life serenely happy; for they were infected by others with the disease, drawing on themselves the sickness of their neighbors and cheerfully accepting their pains. Many, in nursing and curing others, transferred their death to themselves and died in their stead.
Dionysisus, writing about the Christians' response to a devastating disease epidemic, around A.D. 260

HEBREWS 12:1-3
Therefore, since we are surrounded by such a great cloud of witnesses, let us throw off everything that hinders and the sin that so easily entangles. And let us run with perseverance the race marked out for us, fixing our eyes on Jesus, the pioneer and perfecter of faith. For the joy set before him he endured the cross, scorning its shame, and sat down at the right hand of the throne of God. Consider him who endured such opposition from sinners, so that you will not grow weary and lose heart.

4.1 Of what value is our sacrifice to God's economy?

4.2 What role does sacrifice play in your business or professional life? Within your family?

4.3 To what end are you sacrificing your time, energy, and wealth?

⨀

Belonging to God places us in his economy. As his sons and daughters, we obtain a new status that supersedes our economic status. Belonging to him, those who are materially poor are actually rich. By contrast, those who have material wealth but no citizenship in God's kingdom might discover that they are spiritually poor.

5. Our status quo, from the world's perspective, is called into question by God's economy. Consider the following Scriptures.

MATTHEW 16:26

What good will it be for someone to gain the whole world, yet forfeit their soul? Or what can anyone give in exchange for their soul?

LUKE 9:24-25

For whoever wants to save their life will lose it, but whoever loses their life for me will save it. What good is it for someone to gain the whole world, and yet lose or forfeit their very self?

2 CORINTHIANS 8:9

For you know the grace of our Lord Jesus Christ, that though he was rich, yet for your sake he became poor, so that you through his poverty might become rich.

JOHN 6:27

Do not work for food that spoils, but for food that endures to eternal life, which the Son of Man will give you. For on him God the Father has placed his seal of approval.

5.1 Who, according to God's economy, is rich? Who is poor?

5.2 Do you see yourself as being rich or poor? Why?

5.3 What must happen in our lives for us to become truly rich?

∽

Just as every nation, company, and family has its own economy, God's economy has certain traits that make it distinct from the world's economies. His economy is an expression of his character, which is love through and through. As the apostle John wrote, "God is love." His love is not tepid or scarce. It is abundant, steadfast, relentless, and unconditional. Out of this overflowing love, God created an abundant material world.

Today, many fail to understand the abundance of God as it pertains to his economy. We often believe that material wealth is a fixed amount, like a pie. We think that whatever one person eats reduces what's left over for others. Or, as one person becomes rich, another by default becomes poorer. This view, called "zero-sum economics," leads us to believe that fairness or justice requires everyone to have the same amount of wealth. That, in turn, can lead to policies that redistribute wealth, taking resources from the wealthy and giving it to the poor.

"Since government produces no goods," writes Herbert Schlossberg, "it can distribute only what it takes from others. This process is indistinguishable from theft. . . . In a redistributive society, law is a thief."

It is important to remember that shifting wealth from one group to another often does nothing to increase the overall wealth of a nation.

God's economy is different. He is infinite, loving, and generous. He designed the material world in such a way that wealth can multiply and grow. Wealth, in the biblical view, is not a fixed sum. In fact, God's economy is based on the attribute of abundance.

6. Consider the abundant material provision of God in the following scriptures.

GENESIS 1:20-25

And God said, "Let the water teem with living creatures, and let birds fly above the earth across the vault of the sky." So God created the great creatures of the sea and every living thing with which the water teems and that moves about in it, according to their kinds, and every winged bird according to its kind. And God saw that it was good. God blessed them and said, "Be fruitful and increase in number and fill the water in the seas, and let the birds increase on the earth." And there was evening, and there was morning—the fifth day. And God said, "Let the land produce living creatures according to their kinds: the livestock, the creatures that move along the ground, and the wild animals, each according to its kind." And it was so. God made the wild animals according to their kinds, the livestock according to their kinds, and all the creatures that move along the ground according to their kinds. And God saw that it was good.

GENESIS 2:9

The Lord God made all kinds of trees grow out of the ground—trees that were pleasing to the eye and good for food.

Is abundance the root cause of corruption, as the following quote implies? If not, what is? "Home to over one billion barrels of oil reserves, Equatorial Guinea has exported as many as 400,000 barrels of oil a day since 1995. . . . Little of this wealth, however, has helped the vast majority of Equatorial Guinea's 700,000 people: today, three out of every four Equatorial Guineans live on less than $2 a day . . . Equatorial Guinea has become a textbook example of the so-called resource curse, a global phenomenon in which vast natural resource wealth leads to rapacious corruption, decimated governance, and chronic underdevelopment."
Larry Diamond and Jack Mosbacher, in Foreign Affairs

PSALM 65:8-13

The whole earth is filled with awe at your wonders; where morning dawns, where evening fades, you call forth songs of joy. You care for the land and water it; you enrich it abundantly. The streams of God are filled with water to provide the people with grain, for so you have ordained it. You drench its furrows and level its ridges; you soften it with showers and bless its crops. You crown the year with your bounty, and your carts overflow with abundance. The grasslands of the wilderness overflow; the hills are clothed with gladness. The meadows are covered with flocks and the valleys are mantled with grain; they shout for joy and sing.

PSALM 104:24-28

How many are your works, Lord! In wisdom you made them all; the earth is full of your creatures. There is the sea, vast and spacious, teeming with creatures beyond number—living things both large and small. There the ships go to and fro, and Leviathan, which you formed to frolic there. All creatures look to you to give them their food at the proper time. When you give it to them, they gather it up; when you open your hand, they are satisfied with good things.

DEUTERONOMY 28:1-14

If you fully obey the Lord your God and carefully follow all his commands I give you today, the Lord your God will set you high above all the nations on earth. All these blessings will come on you and accompany you if you obey the Lord your God: You will be blessed in the city and blessed in the country. The fruit of your womb will be blessed, and the crops of your land and the young of your livestock—the calves of your herds and the lambs of your flocks. Your basket and your kneading trough will be blessed. You will be blessed when you come in and blessed when you go out. The Lord will grant that the enemies who rise up against you will be defeated before you. They will come at you from one direction but flee from you in seven. The Lord will send a blessing on your barns and on everything you put your hand to. The Lord your God will bless you in the land he is giving you. The Lord will establish you as his holy people, as he promised you on oath, if you keep the commands of the Lord your God and walk in obedience to him.

Then all the peoples on earth will see that you are called by the name of the Lord, and they will fear you. The Lord will grant you abundant prosperity—in the fruit of your womb, the young of your livestock and the crops of your ground—in the land he swore to your ancestors to give you. The Lord will open the heavens, the storehouse of his bounty, to send rain on your land in season and to bless all the work of your hands. You will lend to many nations but will borrow from none. The Lord will make you the head, not the tail. If you pay attention to the commands of the Lord your God that I give you this day and carefully follow them, you will always be at the top, never at the bottom. Do not turn aside from any of the commands I give you today, to the right or to the left, following other gods and serving them.

6.1 If God's provision is so abundant, why does the world deal with so much scarcity?

6.2 What are some causes of inequality? Is wealth inequality unfair?

~

There was no hint of scarcity in Eden, or in all of God's creation. The means of life and productivity were freely available with the assumption that these resources were abundant, able to be multiplied and renewed to supply all generations.

As we have seen in this section, the economy of God operates on a different value system than the world's economies. Paul expresses these distinctions well in a letter he wrote to his friend Timothy.

"But godliness with contentment is great gain. For we brought nothing into the world, and we can take nothing out of it. But if we have food and clothing, we will be content with that. Those who want to get rich fall into temptation and a trap and into many foolish and harmful desires that plunge people into ruin and destruction. For the love of money is a root of all kinds of evil. Some people, eager for money, have wandered from the faith and pierced themselves with many griefs. But you, man of God, flee from all this, and pursue righteousness, godliness, faith, love, endurance and gentleness.

"Fight the good fight of the faith. Take hold of the eternal life to which you were called when you made your good confession in the presence of many witnesses. . . . Command those who are rich in this present world not to be arrogant nor to put their hope in wealth, which is so uncertain, but to put their hope in God, who richly provides us with everything for our enjoyment. Command them to do good, to be rich in good deeds, and to be generous and willing to share. In this way they will lay up treasure for themselves as a firm foundation for the coming age, so that they may take hold of the life that is truly life" (1 Timothy 6:6-12, 17-19).

SECTION NOTES

SECTION 2
CAPITAL

The material world is not just the home in which we live, the classroom where we learn, and a dazzling delight to our senses, it is also the means by which people can sustain themselves and serve others. An incredible gift from God, this earth is an abundant resource that can attend to our material needs. These resources, because they continue to produce and multiply, are called "capital." As we know, capital is necessary to the health of any enterprise, family, and nation.

The importance and legitimacy of capital is solidly established in the Scriptures. Renowned historian Rodney Stark demonstrates that a benevolent capitalism would never have emerged had it not been for the rise of the Christian worldview after the Roman era. A love-motivated and well-managed capitalism began with the rise of hard working, industrious monks who set up monasteries to serve local communities in medieval times.

"In contrast with Eastern holy men, for example, who specialize in meditation and live by charity, medieval Christian monastics lived by their own labor, sustaining highly productive estates," writes Rodney Stark. "Thus it was that, beginning in about the ninth century, the growing monastic estates came to resemble well-organized and stable firms that pursued complex commercial activities within a relatively free market, investing in productive activities involving a hired workforce, guided by anticipated and actual returns."

Capital comes from the Latin word, *caput,* which means "head" or "life." *Capitalis* is the adjective form. The term itself suggests its important role in economic life. Today, we define capital as any asset that produces an ongoing benefit or return. Capital functions like a tree that year after year produces seeds and fruit, multiplying itself and generating ongoing benefits.

Capital is often used interchangeably with the word "asset," which comes from the Latin, *ad satis,* to have sufficiency. "Satisfaction" comes from this root. The idea is that there is enough to satisfy our needs. An understanding of capital and how it works is a foundational element in the economy of God.

Capital comes in many forms. Various types of capital have always ex-

isted but successive periods of economic history have emphasized one type
or another as being most significant.

The first type is **material capital**. This consists of land, cash, a business, tools, and other physical materials. Since the beginning of history,
material capital has always come initially as an inheritance, a purchase,
work, or by conquest. The crops or minerals taken from the land were consumed or stored. Tools were developed to assist in the process. This largely
characterized the Agricultural Age.

Tools were refined into machines, equipment, factories, and new forms
of infrastructure during the Industrial Age. The ability to create a return
became based on technological capital whether it was Gutenberg's printing
press, McCormick's reaper, or Ford's production line. This age moved man
from a focus on extraction of commodities to the manufacture of goods.
Our role also changed as machines took over significant aspects of work.

Human capital consists of resources such as health and education.
Athletic talents and academic prowess can be forms of human capital.
One's relationships play an important role in the context of human capital.

Today's Information Age is driven by **intellectual capital.** It consists
of ideas and information. It produces innovation, knowledge, images, and
research. The productivity of the Information Age has produced a phenom-
enal surplus of intellectual property and services.

The **scarcest form of capital is time** – your time, your attention.
Time is not only a form of capital, it is also the necessary factor for capital
to multiply. A seed takes time to become a fruit producing tree. The sooner
we save some of our income, the larger our nest egg can grow.

The intended result of capital in all its forms is some form of return,
or income. Income is distinct from capital, and it is crucial to understand
the difference between the two. If we treat capital as income, we will erode
wealth and the ability to produce income in the future. Income derives from
a word that means "arrival, entrance, or beginning." It has come to mean
the earnings from one's work. Income can be derived from two primary
sources: a yield from an investment and the wages of labor. The owner of
the orchard (the capital) derives a harvest (the income) from his fruit trees.

7. Observe in the following scriptures the kinds of capital God has endowed us with.

GENESIS 1: 29-30
  Then God said, "I give you every seed-bearing plant on the face of the whole
earth and every tree that has fruit with seed in it. They will be yours for food. And
to all the beasts of the earth and all the birds in the sky and all the creatures that

move along the ground—everything that has the breath of life in it—I give every green plant for food." And it was so.

GENESIS 2:12
The gold of that land is good; aromatic resin and onyx are also there.

The term 'capital' came into use in the fourteenth century to identify funds having the capacity to return income, rather than simply being of consumable value. Thus, in early usage, 'capitalism' referred to the use of wealth (or money) to earn wealth (or money). *Rodney Stark*

GENESIS 4:22
Zillah also had a son, Tubal-Cain, who forged all kinds of tools out of bronze and iron. Tubal-Cain's sister was Naamah.

GENESIS 9:20
Noah, a man of the soil, proceeded to plant a vineyard.

GENESIS 13:2
Abram had become very wealthy in livestock and in silver and gold.

GENESIS 26:12-16
Isaac planted crops in that land and the same year reaped a hundredfold, because the Lord blessed him. The man became rich, and his wealth continued to grow until he became very wealthy. He had so many flocks and herds and servants that the Philistines envied him. So all the wells that his father's servants had dug in the time of his father Abraham, the Philistines stopped up, filling them with earth. Then Abimelek said to Isaac, "Move away from us; you have become too powerful for us."

One of the traits that makes humans unique, different from animals, is our ability to use our skills and talents to shape material things to reflect our individuality. And when we do this, we create property. Material things in and of themselves are not property; they become property only when humans creatively find ways to use them productively. An example is sticky, black, smelly substance that was nothing but a nuisance until humans developed technology for refining it—then, suddenly, oil became a source of wealth. Seen in this light, the defense of the right to property is not a defense of material things per se, but rather of the dignity of human creativity, ingenuity, and inventiveness. *Charles Colson*

PSALM 104:5-30
He set the earth on its foundations; it can never be moved. You covered it with the watery depths as with a garment; the waters stood above the mountains. But at your rebuke the waters fled, at the sound of your thunder they took to flight;

they flowed over the mountains, they went down into the valleys, to the place you assigned for them.

You set a boundary they cannot cross; never again will they cover the earth. He makes springs pour water into the ravines; it flows between the mountains. They give water to all the beasts of the field; the wild donkeys quench their thirst. The birds of the sky nest by the waters; they sing among the branches. He waters the mountains from his upper chambers; the land is satisfied by the fruit of his work.

He makes grass grow for the cattle, and plants for people to cultivate—bringing forth food from the earth: wine that gladdens human hearts, oil to make their faces shine, and bread that sustains their hearts.The trees of the Lord are well watered, the cedars of Lebanon that he planted. There the birds make their nests; the stork has its home in the junipers. The high mountains belong to the wild goats; the crags are a refuge for the hyrax.

He made the moon to mark the seasons, and the sun knows when to go down. You bring darkness, it becomes night, and all the beasts of the forest prowl. The lions roar for their prey and seek their food from God. The sun rises, and they steal away; they return and lie down in their dens. Then people go out to their work, to their labor until evening. How many are your works, Lord!

In wisdom you made them all; the earth is full of your creatures. There is the sea, vast and spacious, teeming with creatures beyond number—living things both large and small. There the ships go to and fro, and Leviathan, which you formed to frolic there. All creatures look to you, to give them their food at the proper time. When you give it to them, they gather it up; when you open your hand, they are satisfied with good things.

When you hide your face, they are terrified; when you take away their breath, they die and return to the dust. When you send your Spirit, they are created, and you renew the face of the ground.

ISAIAH 45:18

For this is what the Lord says—he who created the heavens, he is God; he who fashioned and made the earth, he founded it; he did not create it to be empty, but formed it to be inhabited—he says: "I am the Lord, and there is no other."

ISAIAH 55: 10-11

As the rain and the snow come down from heaven, and do not return to it without watering the earth and making it bud and flourish, so that it yields seed for the sower and bread for the eater, so is my word that goes out from my mouth: It will not return to me empty, but will accomplish what I desire.

> Notions such as the dignity of labor or the idea that work is a virtuous activity were incomprehensible in ancient Rome or in any other precapitalist society. . . . Conversely, capitalism seems to require and to encourage a remarkably different attitude toward work—to see it as intrinsically virtuous and also to recognize the virtue of restricting one's consumption. *Rodney Stark*

PSALM 90:10-17
Our days may come to seventy years, or eighty, if our strength endures; yet the best of them are but trouble and sorrow, for they quickly pass, and we fly away. If only we knew the power of your anger! Your wrath is as great as the fear that is your due. Teach us to number our days that we may gain a heart of wisdom. Relent, Lord! How long will it be? Have compassion on your servants. Satisfy us in the morning with your unfailing love that we may sing for joy and be glad all our days. Make us glad for as many days as you have afflicted us, for as many years as we have seen trouble. May your deeds be shown to your servants, your splendor to their children. May the favor of the Lord our God rest on us; establish the work of our hands for us—yes, establish the work of our hands.

7.1 What importance do you place on capital in your personal and business thinking?

7.2 Which of these forms of capital is subject to scarcity? Which is abundant?

7.3 Which of these can be created? Which need to be managed?

⤗

God delivered the nation of Israel out of slavery in Egypt, where they had lived for 430 years. However, because of their rebellion against God, what should have been a journey of a couple of months to a permanent home turned out to be forty years of wandering in a desert. During this time, God miraculously provided food and other essentials for them each day. As the nation was about to enter the land, God gave each tribal family a piece of land as its possession. God was giving them capital.

8. For almost forty years, the Israelites lived on God's welfare provision. This was not God's long-term intention. What did God provide to replace the temporary welfare situation? The following Scriptures address this question.

DEUTERONOMY 8:1-20
Be careful to follow every command I am giving you today, so that you may live and increase and may enter and possess the land the Lord promised on oath

to your ancestors. Remember how the Lord your God led you all the way in the
wilderness these forty years, to humble and test you in order to know what was
in your heart, whether or not you would keep his commands. He humbled you,
causing you to hunger and then feeding you with manna, which neither you nor
your ancestors had known, to teach you that man does not live on bread alone but
on every word that comes from the mouth of the Lord. Your clothes did not wear
out and your feet did not swell during these forty years. Know then in your heart
that as a man disciplines his son, so the Lord your God disciplines you. Observe the
commands of the Lord your God, walking in obedience to him and revering him.

For the Lord your God is bringing you into a good land—a land with brooks,
streams, and deep springs gushing out into the valleys and hills; a land with wheat
and barley, vines and fig trees, pomegranates, olive oil and honey; a land where
bread will not be scarce and you will lack nothing; a land where the rocks are iron
and you can dig copper out of the hills. When you have eaten and are satisfied,
praise the Lord your God for the good land he has given you.

Be careful that you do not forget the Lord your God, failing to observe his commands, his laws and his decrees that I am giving you this day. Otherwise, when you
eat and are satisfied, when you build fine houses and settle down, and when your
herds and flocks grow large and your silver and gold increase and all you have is
multiplied, then your heart will become proud and you will forget the Lord your
God, who brought you out of Egypt, out of the land of slavery. He led you through
the vast and dreadful wilderness, that thirsty and waterless land, with its venom-
ous snakes and scorpions. He brought you water out of hard rock. He gave you
manna to eat in the wilderness, something your ancestors had never known, to
humble and test you so that in the end it might go well with you.

You may say to yourself, "My power and the strength of my hands have produced this wealth for me." But remember the Lord your God, for it is he who gives
you the ability to produce wealth, and so confirms his covenant, which he swore to
your ancestors, as it is today. If you ever forget the Lord your God and follow other
gods and worship and bow down to them, I testify against you today that you will
surely be destroyed. Like the nations the Lord destroyed before you, so you will be
destroyed for not obeying the Lord your God.

> While the production and consumption of material things is not what life is
> about, it is important to recognize that they are necessary conditions to what
> human life ultimately means. Without material needs being satisfied, humans
> cannot carry out God's mission and realize their spiritual potential. For this
> reason, the material means themselves must be created, protected, and
> sustained. *Rodney Wilson*

JOSHUA 1:1-16

After the death of Moses the servant of the Lord, the Lord said to Joshua son of
Nun, Moses' aide: "Moses my servant is dead. Now then, you and all these people,
get ready to cross the Jordan River into the land I am about to give to them—to the
Israelites. I will give you every place where you set your foot, as I promised Mo-

ses. Your territory will extend from the desert to Lebanon, and from the great river, the Euphrates—all the Hittite country—to the Mediterranean Sea in the west. No one will be able to stand against you all the days of your life. As I was with Moses, so I will be with you; I will never leave you nor forsake you. Be strong and courageous, because you will lead these people to inherit the land I swore to their ancestors to give them.

8.1 What attitudes and actions of the people had to change as Israel's economy moved from the welfare system in the desert to an economy based on capital?

8.2 What did God expect in return for his provision of capital to his people?

8.3 What differences does capital make in a family's economy?

☙

This earth is an extraordinary base of capital, not on loan to us, but given to us by God. We are responsible for managing this capital and utilizing it in order to carry out God's purposes for us. Understanding this enables us to exercise initiative and creativity towards that end.

We must, however, avoid the thinking, habits and actions that erode or squander our capital. We must understand the relationship between capital and income. And we must understand that a long-term perspective is required to grow capital. This capital, properly cared for, will not only provide resources and opportunities for our needs but also provide us with the freedom to fully live our lives in the image of God.

9. There are many threats to sustaining capital. The following scriptures portray some of these threats.

GENESIS 47:17-20

So they brought their livestock to Joseph, and he gave them food in exchange for their horses, their sheep and goats, their cattle and donkeys. And he brought them through that year with food in exchange for all their livestock. When that year was over, they came to him the following year and said, "We cannot hide from our lord the fact that since our money is gone and our livestock belongs to you, there is nothing left for our lord except our bodies and our land. Why should we perish before your eyes—we and our land as well? Buy us and our land in exchange for food, and we with our land will be in bondage to Pharaoh. Give us seed so that we may live and not die, and that the land may not become desolate." So Joseph bought all the land in Egypt for Pharaoh. The Egyptians, one and all, sold their fields, because the famine was too severe for them. The land became Pharaoh's.

EXODUS 20:17

You shall not covet your neighbor's house. You shall not covet your neighbor's wife, or his male or female servant, his ox or donkey, or anything that belongs to your neighbor.

EXODUS 22:8-12

But if the thief is not found, the owner of the house must appear before the judges, and they must determine whether the owner of the house has laid hands on the other person's property. In all cases of illegal possession of an ox, a donkey, a sheep, a garment, or any other lost property about which somebody says, 'This is mine,' both parties are to bring their cases before the judges. The one whom the judges declare guilty must pay back double to the other. If anyone gives a donkey, an ox, a sheep or any other animal to their neighbor for safekeeping and it dies or is injured or is taken away while no one is looking, the issue between them will be settled by the taking of an oath before the Lord that the neighbor did not lay hands on the other person's property. The owner is to accept this, and no restitution is required. But if the animal was stolen from the neighbor, restitution must be made to the owner.

> From the earliest days of the settlement, the American colonists invested heavily in 'human capital,' as modern economists would put it. And in this, religion played a primary role. . . . Only sixteen years after landing at Plymouth Rock, the Puritans founded Harvard. . . . Prior to the (American) Revolution, ten institutions of higher learning had already begun operating in the American colonies. . . . Of these, only the University of Pennsylvania, instituted by Benjamin Franklin to train businessmen, was not affiliated with a denomination. *Rodney Stark, writing about education as human capital*

PROVERBS 6:1-10

My son, if you have put up security for your neighbor or if you have shaken hands in pledge for a stranger, you have been trapped by what you said, ensnared by the words of your mouth. So do this, my son, to free yourself, since you have fallen into your neighbor's hands: Go—to the point of exhaustion—and give your neighbor no rest! Allow no sleep to your eyes, no slumber to your eyelids. Free yourself, like a gazelle from the hand of the hunter, like a bird from the snare of the fowler. Go to the ant, you sluggard; consider its ways and be wise! It has no commander, no overseer or ruler, yet it stores its provisions in summer and gathers its food at harvest. How long will you lie there, you sluggard? When will you get up from your sleep?

PROVERBS 24:30-34

I went past the field of a sluggard, past the vineyard of someone who has no sense; thorns had come up everywhere, the ground was covered with weeds, and the stone wall was in ruins. I applied my heart to what I observed and learned a lesson from what I saw: A little sleep, a little slumber a little folding of the hands to rest—and poverty will come on you like a thief and scarcity like an armed man.

> In order to navigate the increasing complexity of the 21st century . . .
> You need to optimize your life for learning. You need to live and breathe
> your education. You need to be obsessed with your education. . . . That
> is why I am not canceling class tomorrow. Your education is really, really
> important, not just to you, but in a far broader and wider reaching way than I
> think any of you have yet to fully appreciate. See you tomorrow.
> *Alexander Coward, math professor at the University of California, Berkeley,*
> *in an email to his students during a university labor strike.*

PROVERBS 27:23-27

Be sure you know the condition of your flocks, give careful attention to your herds; or riches do not endure forever, and a crown is not secure for all generations. When the hay is removed and new growth appears and the grass from the hills is gathered in, the lambs will provide you with clothing, and the goats with the price of a field. You will have plenty of goats' milk to feed you and your family and to nourish your servant girls.

NEHEMIAH 5:1-13

Now the men and their wives raised a great outcry against their fellow Jews. Some were saying, "We and our sons and daughters are numerous; in order for us to eat and stay alive, we must get grain."

Others were saying, "We are mortgaging our fields, our vineyards and our homes to get grain during the famine."

Still others were saying, "We have had to borrow money to pay the king's tax on our fields and vineyards. Although we are of the same flesh and blood as our fellow Jews and though our children are as good as theirs, yet we have to subject our sons and daughters to slavery. Some of our daughters have already been enslaved, but we are powerless, because our fields and our vineyards belong to others."

When I heard their outcry and these charges, I was very angry. I pondered them in my mind and then accused the nobles and officials. I told them, "You are charging your own people interest!"

So I called together a large meeting to deal with them and said: "As far as possible, we have bought back our fellow Jews who were sold to the Gentiles. Now you are selling your own people, only for them to be sold back to us!" They kept quiet, because they could find nothing to say.

So I continued, "What you are doing is not right. Shouldn't you walk in the fear of our God to avoid the reproach of our Gentile enemies? I and my brothers and my men are also lending the people money and grain. But let us stop charging interest! Give back to them immediately their fields, vineyards, olive groves and houses, and also the interest you are charging them—one percent of the money, grain, new wine and olive oil."

"We will give it back," they said. "And we will not demand anything more from them. We will do as you say."

Then I summoned the priests and made the nobles and officials take an oath to do what they had promised. I also shook out the folds of my robe and said, "In this way may God shake out of their house and possessions anyone who does not keep this promise. So may such a person be shaken out and emptied!"

At this the whole assembly said, "Amen," and praised the Lord. And the people did as they had promised.

LEVITICUS 25:23-25

The land must not be sold permanently, because the land is mine and you reside in my land as foreigners and strangers. Throughout the land that you hold as a possession, you must provide for the redemption of the land. If one of your fellow Israelites becomes poor and sells some of their property, their nearest relative is to come and redeem what they have sold.

> . . . industrial capitalism, contrary to Marx, was not bound by any historical destiny to produce poverty, class conflict, and ruthless business competition. Such consequences arose from human pride and irresponsibility, in a word, from sin. *Glenn Tinder*

GALATIANS 6:7-9

Do not be deceived: God cannot be mocked. A man reaps what he sows. Whoever sows to please their flesh, from the flesh will reap destruction; whoever sows to please the Spirit, from the Spirit will reap eternal life. Let us not become weary in doing good, for at the proper time we will reap a harvest if we do not give up.

9.1 Among the threats to the preservation of capital described above, which are most dangerous for you? Can you think of additional threats to the preservation of capital?

9.2 How are you proactive in preserving your capital?

With resources comes stewardship. God gives people real ownership, relationships, and consequences. Our initiative, our work, and our efforts matter. Our creativity and responsibility are made possible through ownership of the resources that God entrusts to us.

There is no disputing that God, as Creator, is the ultimate owner of all things. The Scriptures say, "The earth is the Lord's and all it contains. . . ." But the Scriptures are clear that God is also the "great giver" and that he has given a great gift of the earth and its resources to man. It is not a loan; it is a gift. We have a responsibility.

There is a school of thought that says we own nothing, that it is all God's. In this view, we are just managers, or perhaps tenant farmers. This would counter, to a certain extent, any pride or wrong-hearted materialism. However, the Scriptures are replete with references to real ownership, not just apparent ownership.

A simple analogy might be this. As a father earns, creates, and purchases possessions, they are his. But that same father can give gifts to his young children. The gifts are his, but he really does give them to the kids. What father gives gifts to his children with the caveat that they are only loaned to them?

In the end, the concept of ownership says less about our relationship to "things" than about God's heart for us! What love! What trust! What risk! How much he entrusts to us! Freedom certainly has its risks. Freedom can be abused and often is. But freedom is a foundational condition for trust.

10. *What do the Scriptures teach us about ownership?*

GENESIS 17:8
The whole land of Canaan, where you are now an alien, I will give as an everlasting possession to you and your descendants after you; and I will be their God.

> . . . the lack of secure title to land inhibits economic development. That lack of title means a lack of access to credit due to lack of collateral. . . . Lack of title also undermines incentives. . . . De Soto (a Peruvian economist) found that investment in home improvements increased nine fold when Peruvian squatters gained title to their homes. *Jeff Gates*

GENESIS 25:5
Abraham left everything he owned to Isaac.

GENESIS 39:4-6

Joseph found favor in his eyes and became his attendant. Potiphar put him in charge of his household, and he entrusted to his care everything he owned. From the time he put him in charge of his household and of all that he owned, the Lord blessed the household of the Egyptian because of Joseph. The blessing of the Lord was on everything Potiphar had, both in the house and in the field. So Potiphar left everything he had in Joseph's care; with Joseph in charge, he did not concern himself with anything except the food he ate.

> . . . people are likely to become better stewards of all those systems of which they are a part—social, political, fiscal, cultural, and natural—as they gain a personal stake in the economic system, with all the rights and responsibilities that implies. . . . As Americans moved off the farm, they became a nation of employees rather than proprietors, becoming wage earners and modern-day sharecroppers rather than equity-empowered stake-owners. That must change. *Jeff Gates*

PSALM 115:16

The highest heavens belong to the LORD, but the earth he has given to man.

DEUTERONOMY 5:19

You shall not steal.

> Why should farmers seek or adopt new and better agricultural technology if all the increased production will be taken from them? Who will reinvest profits to expand an industry if it is apt to be expropriated by the nobility? Invention and innovation tend to occur only where property is safe from seizure either because the state has become disorganized or because its powers have been curtailed. *Rodney Stark*

ACTS 4:36-37 AND ACTS 5:4

Joseph, a Levite from Cyprus, whom the apostles called Barnabas (which means Son of Encouragement), sold a field he owned and brought the money and put it at the apostles' feet. . . .

"Didn't it belong to you before it was sold? And after it was sold, wasn't the money at your disposal? What made you think of doing such a thing? You have not lied to men but to God."

10.1 Why is protecting the ownership rights of property so important?

10.2 How do the freedoms, constraints, initiatives, and responsibilities of an owner differ from those of a manager?

10.3 God is constantly trying to develop maturity, freedom, and ability in people to live out his purposes. Does helping people become owners enhance or hinder this?

∽

John Bradford of the Plymouth Colony quickly discovered that private ownership of property led people to produce better and more, in effect creating a surplus from which the capital and the capabilities of people could grow. When all shared equally in the ownership, irrespective of their work, productivity was down, and initiative was down.

God gives people real ownership, real opportunity, and real consequences. Our creativity and our responsibility are enhanced by the ownership of the resources which God entrusts to us.

11. We are also called to be managers, stewards. Whereas ownership says much about our relationship to God, stewardship speaks to our task. What are the expectations placed upon a steward?

MATTHEW 25:14-30

Again, it will be like a man going on a journey, who called his servants and entrusted his property to them. To one he gave five talents of money, to another two talents, and to another one talent, each according to his ability. Then he went on his journey. The man who had received the five talents went at once and put his money to work and gained five more. So also, the one with the two talents gained two more. But the man who had received the one talent went off, dug a hole in the ground and hid his master's money.

After a long time the master of those servants returned and settled accounts with them. The man who had received the five talents brought the other five. 'Master,' he said, 'you entrusted me with five talents. See, I have gained five more.'

His master replied, 'well done, good and faithful servant! You have been faithful with a few things; I will put you in charge of many things. Come and share your master's happiness!'

The man with the two talents also came. 'Master,' he said, 'you entrusted me with two talents; see, I have gained two more.'

His master replied, 'well done, good and faithful servant! You have been faithful with a few things; I will put you in charge of many things. Come and share your master's happiness!' For even though you have received an inheritance from your father, and have in this way come to possess everything you have, still everything belongs to God. . . .

Therefore though he could have taken these possessions away from you, God left them so that you may have the opportunity to show forth virtue. Thus, bringing us into need one of another, he makes our love for one another more fervent.*St. John Chrysostom (A.D. 347-407)*

. . . Then the man who had received the one talent came. 'Master,' he said, 'I knew that you are a hard man, harvesting where you have not sown and gathering where you have not scattered seed. So I was afraid and went out and hid your talent in the ground. See, here is what belongs to you.'

His master replied, 'you wicked, lazy servant! So you knew that I harvest where I have not sown and gather where I have not scattered seed? Well then, you should have put my money on deposit with the bankers, so that when I returned I would have received it back with interest.

'Take the talent from him and give it to the one who has the ten talents. For everyone who has will be given more, and he will have an abundance. Whoever does not have, even what he has will be taken from him. And throw that worthless servant outside, into the darkness, where there will be weeping and gnashing of teeth.'

Stewardship functions in relationship to capital. Good stewards preserve their capital, increase it, and manage it in such a way that it produces continuing benefits. Good stewardship is a sign of economic maturity and leads to innumerable benefits. These benefits include the satisfaction of assuming responsibility, the privilege of providing for family, the experience of growth and enterprise, and—most significantly—the opportunity for giving. *Jake Barnett*

LUKE 12: 41-48

Peter asked, "Lord, are you telling this parable to us, or to everyone?"

The Lord answered, "Who then is the faithful and wise manager, whom the master puts in charge of his servants to give them their food allowance at the proper time? It will be good for that servant whom the master finds doing so when he returns. I tell you the truth, he will put him in charge of all his possessions. But suppose the servant says to himself, 'My master is taking a long time in coming,' and he then begins to beat the menservants and maidservants and to eat and drink and get drunk. The master of that servant will come on a day when he does not expect him and at an hour he is not aware of. He will cut him to pieces and assign him a place with the unbelievers. That servant who knows his master's will and does not get ready or does not do what his master wants will be beaten with many blows. But the one who does not know and does things deserving punishment will be beaten with few blows. From everyone who has been given much, much will be demanded; and from the one who has been entrusted with much, much more will be asked."

(In the Jewish and Christian view), The resources of the earth are held in trust for a divine purpose. Thus our relationship to money and property may by custom or law be defined as ownership but is really a conditional form of trusteeship. In the true sense of the Old English word 'steward,' we are responsible for the prudent management of an estate that is not our own.
Os Guinness

1 PETER 4:10
Each one should use whatever gift he has received to serve others, faithfully administering God's grace in its various forms.

11.1 What are the expectations placed upon a steward?

11.2 How does the fact that you are made in the image of God and an heir to the kingdom of God expand the way you think about the concept of stewardship?

We have an extraordinary base of capital. We are responsible for growing this capital and utilizing it in order to carry out the purposes of God. Understanding this enables us to exercise initiative and creativity in carrying out our responsibilities and our purpose. It also helps us integrate our work and economic lives with the grand plans of God. This is key to living a meaningful, fruitful life in the context of a complex, broken world.

We must, however, avoid the thinking, habits, and actions that erode or squander our capital. We must understand the relationship of capital and income. And we must understand that a long-term perspective is required to grow capital. Properly cared for, capital will not only provide resources and opportunities for our needs but also provide us with the freedom to fully live our lives in the image of God.

And ultimately, time is our most valuable resource. It is the scarcest and the most perishable. But it is also the resource that connects us to eternity.

SECTION NOTES

SECTION 3
WEALTH AND POVERTY

In the previous sections, we have seen that the kingdom of God has its own economy–the economy of God. Everything in God's economy finds meaning in God's love for people. It includes those who are materially rich and those who are materially poor. Within God's economy, the rich might discover they are in fact spiritually poor, and those who are materially poor can be spiritually rich. In this way, God's economy transcends the world's economies.

God's values are distinct from the world's values. Like oil and water, his design for life often doesn't blend with the cultures and economies designed by us. His ways are not our ways. Thus, anyone who lives according to God's economic design will experience tension with the world. How do we live and work as members of God's economy in a world that is constructed on human foundations?

One common approach is to isolate ourselves within "Christian" subcultures, or to be passive in the public sphere. Another common approach is to "go with the flow," adopting the world's ways without ever questioning how God wants us to engage with commerce and professional life. Both approaches make us ineffective, restricting our ability to fulfill our calling. By contrast, our goal should be to imitate what Jesus modeled: to be deeply engaged with the world while remaining true to our identity in Christ, to his principles, and to his values.

Fortunately, through the Scriptures, God provides us with the wisdom and discernment we need to be engaged in the world's economy and commerce as representatives of God. This study is designed to help us accomplish that profound calling in the context of work and life.

In this section, we deal with two topics that create tremendous debate and confusion: wealth and poverty. Wealth itself can create heart wrenching tension. On the one hand, God has declared that the material wealth he created—a form of capital—is "very good." But the Bible is also full of warnings about the dangers of wealth. It can ruin us. Likewise, poverty also creates tension. If God has created such abundance, why are so many people poor? How are we to respond to poverty?

In Section 1, we addressed the difference between material and spiritual poverty. The Bible makes it very clear that those who are spiritually poor without Christ, even if they have great material wealth, are indeed destitute. The richest man on the planet, without Jesus, is actually impoverished. By contrast, an impoverished person who has salvation through Christ is, in fact, wealthy beyond imagination.

God's concern with our spiritual wealth, however, does not mean that he is uncaring about our material needs. He cares deeply about the material needs of the poor. The Scriptures, as we will see, are full of wisdom designed to help us handle material wealth and avoid poverty.

God's compassion for the poor is visible throughout the Scriptures. Although the Bible does not *guarantee* that the poor will escape physical poverty in this life, the gospel does provide the essential spiritual and relational foundations needed for that to occur.

First, the gospel of Jesus provides the dignity and hope that the poor so desperately need. Grace confirms that every person is valuable to God regardless of economic status, physical condition, race, or age. In Christ, we have a new status as children of God and members of an eternal, righteous kingdom.

Second, new believers can enter a Christian community that provides a loving set of relationships. This community empowers the poor, giving them greater security and stability in the midst of hardship. The relational accountability helps people grow out of self-destructive behaviors. Third, through the Scriptures, God also provides the wisdom needed for making good financial and life decisions. In short, Jesus offers the opportunity to flourish in this life and the next.

12. Read the following Scriptures focusing on God's heart for the poor.

PSALM 82:3-4

Defend the weak and the fatherless; uphold the cause of the poor and the oppressed. Rescue the weak and the needy; deliver them from the hand of the wicked.

> The New Testament taught that God saw the misery of man and came as a man, Jesus Christ, to make human beings sons and daughters of God.
> *Vishal Mangalwadi*

PROVERBS 22:16

One who oppresses the poor to increase his wealth and one who gives gifts to the rich—both come to poverty.

Since human worth is measured in spiritual, not in physical, terms, we ignore our various physical situations: slaves are not slaves to us, but we treat them and address them as brothers in the spirit, fellow slaves in devotion to God. Wealth, too, is no ground for distinction, except insofar as it provides the opportunity for preeminence in good works. To be rich is not a matter of having, but of using riches for the tasks of justice.
Lactantius, third century theologian, in his Divine Institutes

PROVERBS 31:8-9

Speak up for those who cannot speak for themselves, for the rights of all who are destitute. Speak up and judge fairly; defend the rights of the poor and needy.

ISAIAH 10:1-2

Woe to those who make unjust laws, to those who issue oppressive decrees, to deprive the poor of their rights and withhold justice from the oppressed of my people, making widows their prey and robbing the fatherless.

The (Christian) insistence on the uniqueness and value of each person . . . was nowhere to be found in the ancient (pre-Christian) world. . . . Plato, for example, had said that a poor man whose sickness made him unable to work any longer should be left to die. Seneca wrote: 'We drown children who at birth are weakly and abnormal.' *Thomas E. Woods, Jr.*

ISAIAH 58:6-12

Is not this the kind of fasting I have chosen: to loose the chains of injustice and untie the cords of the yoke, to set the oppressed free and break every yoke? Is it not to share your food with the hungry and to provide the poor wanderer with shelter—when you see the naked, to clothe them, and not to turn away from your own flesh and blood? Then your light will break forth like the dawn, and your healing will quickly appear; then your righteousness will go before you, and the glory of the Lord will be your rear guard. Then you will call, and the Lord will answer; you will cry for help, and he will say: Here am I.

If you do away with the yoke of oppression, with the pointing finger and malicious talk, and if you spend yourselves in behalf of the hungry and satisfy the needs of the oppressed, then your light will rise in the darkness, and your night will become like the noonday. The Lord will guide you always; he will satisfy your needs in a sun-scorched land and will strengthen your frame.

You will be like a well-watered garden, like a spring whose waters never fail. Your people will rebuild the ancient ruins and will raise up the age-old foundations; you will be called Repairer of Broken Walls, Restorer of Streets with Dwellings.

12.1 If God has such a compassionate heart for the poor, why is there so much poverty in the world?

12.2 Based on your experience and observations, what are some causes of poverty?

∽

Throughout history there have been unjust commercial practices and structures that hold people in poverty. One recurrent example is slavery. During the first century, the early Christian church had to confront the issue of slavery. The apostle Paul confronted the issue, as recorded in the following letter he wrote to his friend, Philemon. And we see numerous other examples of New Testament writings about slaves.

13. What can we learn from these scriptures about serving the poor today?

PHILEMON 1:1-21

Paul, a prisoner of Christ Jesus, and Timothy our brother, to Philemon our dear friend and fellow worker—also to Apphia our sister and Archippus our fellow soldier—and to the church that meets in your home: Grace and peace to you from God our Father and the Lord Jesus Christ.

I always thank my God as I remember you in my prayers, because I hear about your love for all his holy people and your faith in the Lord Jesus. I pray that your partnership with us in the faith may be effective in deepening your understanding of every good thing we share for the sake of Christ. Your love has given me great joy and encouragement, because you, brother, have refreshed the hearts of the Lord's people.

Therefore, although in Christ I could be bold and order you to do what you ought to do, yet I prefer to appeal to you on the basis of love. It is as none other than Paul—an old man and now also a prisoner of Christ Jesus—that I appeal to you for my son Onesimus, who became my son while I was in chains. Formerly he was useless to you, but now he has become useful both to you and to me. I am sending him—who is my very heart—back to you. I would have liked to keep him with me so that he could take your place in helping me while I am in chains for the gospel.

But I did not want to do anything without your consent, so that any favor you do would not seem forced but would be voluntary. Perhaps the reason he was separated from you for a little while was that you might have him back forever—no longer as a slave, but better than a slave, as a dear brother. He is very dear to me but even dearer to you, both as a fellow man and as a brother in the Lord.

So if you consider me a partner, welcome him as you would welcome me. If he has done you any wrong or owes you anything, charge it to me. I, Paul, am writing this with my own hand. I will pay it back—not to mention that you owe me your very self. I do wish, brother, that I may have some benefit from you in the Lord; refresh my heart in Christ. Confident of your obedience, I write to you, knowing that you will do even more than I ask.

> Jesus asserted a revolutionary conception of moral equality, not only in words but in deeds. Over and over again he ignored major status boundaries [common in the Greco-Roman era] and associated with stigmatized people, including Samaritans, publicans, immoral women, beggars, and various other outcasts, thereby giving divine sanction to spiritual inclusiveness.
> *Rodney Stark*

1 CORINTHIANS 7:21-23

Were you a slave when you were called? Don't let it trouble you—although if you can gain your freedom, do so. For the one who was a slave when called to faith in the Lord is the Lord's freed person; similarly, the one who was free when called is Christ's slave. You were bought at a price; do not become slaves of human beings.

GALATIANS 4:4-7

But when the set time had fully come, God sent his Son, born of a woman, born under the law, to redeem those under the law, that we might receive adoption to sonship. Because you are his sons, God sent the Spirit of his Son into our hearts, the Spirit who calls out, "Abba, Father." So you are no longer a slave, but God's child; and since you are his child, God has made you also an heir.

> The Indians themselves indeed are true men. . . . By our Apostolic authority [we] decree and declare . . . that the same Indians and all other peoples— even though they are outside the faith . . . should not be deprived of their liberty or their possessions . . . and are not reduced to slavery . . ."
> *Pope Paul III, 1537, in a decree condemning Indian slavery in South America*

EPHESIANS 6:5-9

Slaves, obey your earthly masters with respect and fear, and with sincerity of heart, just as you would obey Christ. Obey them not only to win their favor when their eye is on you, but as slaves of Christ, doing the will of God from your heart. Serve wholeheartedly, as if you were serving the Lord, not people, because you know that the Lord will reward each one for whatever good they do, whether they are slave or free. And masters, treat your slaves in the same way. Do not threaten them, since you know that he who is both their Master and yours is in heaven, and there is no favoritism with him.

COLOSSIANS 4:1
Masters, provide your slaves with what is right and fair, because you know that you also have a Master in heaven.

13.1 How did Paul's love for God impact the life of Onesimus (the slave)?

13.2 What status as a person did Onesimus find within the Christian community?

13.3 What do these instructions do to the institution of slavery?

13.4 How do these scriptures help us serve the poor?

14. As you read the following passages, consider what our responsibilities are in relation to the poor.

LEVITICUS 19:9–10
When you reap the harvest of your land, do not reap to the very edges of your field or gather the gleanings of your harvest. Do not go over your vineyard a second time or pick up the grapes that have fallen. Leave them for the poor and the alien. I am the LORD your God.

> There are essentially four different causes of poverty mentioned in the Bible, each kind demanding a different reaction from the Christian. . . . These four different causes of poverty are slothfulness, calamity, exploitation, and personal sacrifice. To lump these four groups together, seeking a common solution, is as foolish as trying to cure cancer, heart disease, the common cold, and insomnia with one pill. *R.C. Sproul*

LEVITICUS 19:15
Do not pervert justice; do not show partiality to the poor or favoritism to the great, but judge your neighbor fairly.

LEVITICUS 25:23–25

If one of your countrymen becomes poor and sells some of his property, his nearest relative is to come and redeem what his countryman has sold.

> Poverty is not a permanent condition, defining the essence of a person, but a circumstance to be assuaged by the restoration of justice or by charitable help until the poor person can resume his normal status in society, one in which he contributes rather than being the recipient of contributions.
> *Herb Schlossberg*

DEUTERONOMY 15:7–11

If there is a poor man among your brothers in any of the towns of the land that the LORD your God is giving you, do not be hardhearted or tightfisted toward your poor brother. Rather be openhanded and freely lend him whatever he needs. Be careful not to harbor this wicked thought: "The seventh year, the year for canceling debts, is near," so that you do not show ill will toward your needy brother and give him nothing. He may then appeal to the LORD against you, and you will be found guilty of sin. Give generously to him and do so without a grudging heart; then because of this the LORD your God will bless you in all your work and in everything you put your hand to. There will always be poor people in the land. Therefore I command you to be openhanded toward your brothers and toward the poor and needy in your land.

> . . . the only dependable route from poverty is always work, family, and faith.
> *George Gilder*

DEUTERONOMY 24:14–15

Do not take advantage of a hired man who is poor and needy, whether he is a brother Israelite or an alien living in one of your towns. Pay him his wages each day before sunset, because he is poor and is counting on it. Otherwise he may cry to the LORD against you, and you will be guilty of sin.

JOB 29:12–16

. . . because I rescued the poor who cried for help, and the fatherless who had none to assist him. The man who was dying blessed me; I made the widow's heart sing. I put on righteousness as my clothing; justice was my robe and my turban. I was eyes to the blind and feet to the lame. I was a father to the needy; I took up the case of the stranger.

> Each time (medieval capitalist firms) drew up or revised a budget, a fund for the poor was created with some of the capital of the company. These funds were entered in the books in the name of 'our Good Lord God' as representing the poor, who in this way were made partners in the company. When dividends were paid, a proportional part went to the poor.
> *Armando Sapori*

PSALM 72:12–14

For he will deliver the needy who cry out, the afflicted who have no one to help. He will take pity on the weak and the needy and save the needy from death. He will rescue them from oppression and violence, for precious is their blood in his sight.

> Justice is related particularly to what is due to groups such as the poor, widows, orphans, resident aliens, wage earners and slaves. The common link among these groups is powerlessness by virtue of economic and social needs. The justice called for is to restore these groups to the provision God intends for them. God's law expressed this justice and indicates His demands. Further, God's intention is for people to live, not in isolation, but in society. The poor are described as those who are weak with respect to the rest of the community. *Oxford Declaration on Christian Faith and Economics*

PSALM 82:3–4

Defend the cause of the weak and fatherless; maintain the rights of the poor and oppressed. Rescue the weak and needy; deliver them from the hand of the wicked.

PROVERBS 14:31

He who oppresses the poor shows contempt for their Maker, but whoever is kind to the needy honors God.

PROVERBS 22:16

He who oppresses the poor to increase his wealth and he who gives gifts to the rich—both come to poverty.

PROVERBS 31:8–9

Speak up for those who cannot speak for themselves, for the rights of all who are destitute. Speak up and judge fairly; defend the rights of the poor and needy.

> By the fourth century, the Church began to sponsor the establishment of hospitals on a large scale, such that nearly every major city had one. These hospitals originally provided hospitality to strangers but eventually cared for the sick, widows, orphans, and the poor in general. . . . Likewise, medical historian Fielding Garrison observes that before the birth of Christ 'the spirit toward sickness and misfortune was not one of compassion, and the credit of ministering to human suffering on an extended scale belongs to Christianity.' *Thomas E. Woods, Jr.*

AMOS 5:11–12

You trample on the poor and force him to give you grain. Therefore, though you have built stone mansions, you will not live in them; though you have planted lush vineyards, you will not drink their wine. For I know how many are your offenses and how great your sins. You oppress the righteous and take bribes and you deprive the poor of justice in the courts.

> Is it, we ask, a very hard-hearted thing for the public to require an equivalent of labor, from those who are able to give it, in return for the relief which they receive? Is it unchristian? Is it not in the sweat of his brow that man is to eat his bread? *Steven Humphreys Gurteen (1840-1898), founder of the Buffalo Charity Organization Society*

2 THESSALONIANS 3:6–10

In the name of the Lord Jesus Christ, we command you, brothers, to keep away from every brother who is idle and does not live according to the teaching you received from us. For you yourselves know how you ought to follow our example. We were not idle when we were with you, nor did we eat anyone's food without paying for it. On the contrary, we worked night and day, laboring and toiling so that we would not be a burden to any of you. We did this, not because we do not have the right to such help, but in order to make ourselves a model for you to follow. For even when we were with you, we gave you this rule: "If a man will not work, he shall not eat."

JAMES 2:1-6

My brothers and sisters, believers in our glorious Lord Jesus Christ must not show favoritism. Suppose a man comes into your meeting wearing a gold ring and fine clothes, and a poor man in filthy old clothes also comes in. If you show special attention to the man wearing fine clothes and say, "Here's a good seat for you," but say to the poor man, "You stand there" or "Sit on the floor by my feet," have you not discriminated among yourselves and become judges with evil thoughts? Listen, my dear brothers and sisters: Has not God chosen those who are poor in the eyes of the world to be rich in faith and to inherit the kingdom he promised those who love him? But you have dishonored the poor. Is it not the rich who are exploiting you? Are they not the ones who are dragging you into court?

1 JOHN 3:16-17

This is how we know what love is: Jesus Christ laid down his life for us. And we ought to lay down our lives for our brothers and sisters. If anyone has material possessions and sees a brother or sister in need but has no pity on them, how can the love of God be in that person?

ROMANS 12:16

Live in harmony with one another. Do not be proud, but be willing to associate with people of low position. Do not be conceited.

14.1 What correlation do you see in the verses above between the identified causes of poverty and the proposed approach?

14.2 How have you served the poor? Do you feel satisfied with your efforts and the outcomes?

15. Not all poverty is caused by external forces such as injustice and corruption. It can also be self-inflicted due to our own bad decisions and attitudes.

PROVERBS 6:6–11

Go to the ant, you sluggard; consider its ways and be wise! It has no commander, no overseer or ruler, yet it stores its provisions in summer and gathers its food at harvest. How long will you lie there, you sluggard? When will you get up from your sleep? A little sleep, a little slumber, a little folding of the hands to rest— and poverty will come on you like a bandit and scarcity like an armed man.

PROVERBS 10:4–5

Lazy hands make a man poor, but diligent hands bring wealth. He who gathers crops in summer is a wise son, but he who sleeps during harvest is a disgraceful son.

PROVERBS 13:18

He who ignores discipline comes to poverty and shame, but whoever heeds correction is honored.

PROVERBS 20:4

A sluggard does not plow in season; at harvest time he looks but finds nothing.

PROVERBS 21:5

The plans of the diligent lead to profit as surely as haste leads to poverty.

In today's globalized, financialized, post-industrial environment, human capital (education, relationships, character) is more important than ever in determining life chances. This makes families more important, . . . As the economist Friedrich Hayek pointed out half a century ago . . ., the main impediment to true equality of opportunity is that there is no substitute for intelligent parents or for an emotionally and culturally nurturing family.
Jerry Z. Muller in Foreign Affairs

PROVERBS 21:17

He who loves pleasure will become poor; whoever loves wine and oil will never be rich.

PROVERBS 28:19

He who works his land will have abundant food, but the one who chases fantasies will have his fill of poverty.

LUKE 12:13–21

Someone in the crowd said to him, "Teacher, tell my brother to divide the inheritance with me."

Jesus replied, "Man, who appointed me a judge or an arbiter between you?" Then he said to them, "Watch out! Be on your guard against all kinds of greed; a man's life does not consist in the abundance of his possessions."

And he told them this parable: "The ground of a certain rich man produced a good crop. He thought to himself, 'What shall I do? I have no place to store my crops.' Then he said, 'This is what I'll do. I will tear down my barns and build bigger ones, and there I will store all my grain and my goods. And I'll say to myself, You have plenty of good things laid up for many years. Take life easy; eat, drink and be merry.'

But God said to him, 'You fool! This very night your life will be demanded from you. Then who will get what you have prepared for yourself?' This is how it will be with anyone who stores up things for himself but is not rich toward God."

Capital that is not invested is consumed, in one way or another. . . . An economy living on capital rather than income resembles a body deprived of nourishment, living off its own tissues and wasting away. But this is not an organism that is starving because of the pressure of external factors beyond its control. It is, rather, suffering from an infantile inability to discipline itself and provide for its future. *Herb Schlossberg*

LUKE 19:11–27

While they were listening to this, he went on to tell them a parable, because he was near Jerusalem and the people thought that the kingdom of God was going to appear at once. He said: "A man of noble birth went to a distant country to have himself appointed king and then to return. So he called ten of his servants and gave them ten minas. 'Put this money to work,' he said, 'until I come back.'

"But his subjects hated him and sent a delegation after him to say, 'We don't want this man to be our king.' He was made king, however, and returned home. Then he sent for the servants to whom he had given the money, in order to find out what they had gained with it.

"The first one came and said, 'Sir, your mina has earned ten more.'

'Well done, my good servant!' his master replied. 'Because you have been trustworthy in a very small matter, take charge of ten cities.'

"The second came and said, 'Sir, your mina has earned five more.'

"His master answered, 'You take charge of five cities.'

"Then another servant came and said, 'Sir, here is your mina; I have kept it laid away in a piece of cloth. I was afraid of you, because you are a hard man. You take out what you did not put in and reap what you did not sow.'

"His master replied, 'I will judge you by your own words, you wicked servant! You knew, did you, that I am a hard man, taking out what I did not put in, and reaping what I did not sow? Why then didn't you put my money on deposit, so that when I came back, I could have collected it with interest?'

"Then he said to those standing by, 'Take his mina away from him and give it to the one who has ten minas.'

'Sir,' they said, 'he already has ten!'

He replied, 'I tell you that to everyone who has, more will be given, but as for the one who has nothing, even what he has will be taken away. But those enemies of mine who did not want me to be king over them—bring them here and kill them in front of me.'"

15.1 What habits in our society jeopardize our economic future?

15.2 Which of these habits are you most susceptible to and why?

15.3 What is the result when a person consumes and destroys their capital rather than preserving and growing their capital? What is the impact on the household in this generation and the generations to come?

∽

The Scriptures are clear from the beginning that material wealth is good. After he created the universe, God declared the world to be "very good." Some of the most godly men and women in the Bible were wealthy. And we see in the Scriptures many portraits of wealthy people giving generously and living for the sake of God's kingdom. But the Scriptures also teach us that the wealthy face dangers. The primary concern is that money would become an idol, supplanting the role of God in our lives.

16. What is a healthy attitude toward wealth? What are the particular privileges and obligations of the wealthy?

1 CHRONICLES 29:12

Wealth and honor come from you; you are the ruler of all things. In your hands are strength and power to exalt and give strength to all.

> The task of guiding and restraining the explosive power of capitalism is daunting. At its core is an unavoidable issue: no one can master money without mastering the meaning of money. . . . The truth is that money is much more than a monetary issue. It was, and is, a spiritual issue. *Os Guinness*

PHILIPPIANS 4:10-13

I rejoiced greatly in the Lord that at last you renewed your concern for me. Indeed, you were concerned, but you had no opportunity to show it. I am not saying this because I am in need, for I have learned to be content whatever the circumstances. I know what it is to be in need, and I know what it is to have plenty. I have learned the secret of being content in any and every situation, whether well fed or hungry, whether living in plenty or in want. I can do all this through him who gives me strength.

JOB 31:24–28

If I have put my trust in gold or said to pure gold, 'You are my security,' if I have rejoiced over my great wealth, the fortune my hands had gained, if I have regarded the sun in its radiance or the moon moving in splendor, so that my heart was secretly enticed and my hand offered them a kiss of homage, then these also would be sins to be judged, for I would have been unfaithful to God on high.

PSALM 119:14

I rejoice in following your statutes as one rejoices in great riches.

PROVERBS 22:4

Humility and the fear of the LORD bring wealth and honor and life.

ISAIAH 55:1-2

Come, all you who are thirsty, come to the waters; and you who have no money, come, buy and eat! Come, buy wine and milk without money and without cost. Why spend money on what is not bread, and your labor on what does not satisfy? Listen, listen to me, and eat what is good, and your soul will delight in the richest of fare.

JEREMIAH 9:23–24

This is what the LORD says: "Let not the wise man boast of his wisdom or the strong man boast of his strength or the rich man boast of his riches, but let him who boasts boast about this: that he understands and knows me, that I am the LORD, who exercises kindness, justice and righteousness on earth, for in these I delight," declares the LORD.

MATTHEW 6:19–34

Do not store up for yourselves treasures on earth, where moth and rust destroy, and where thieves break in and steal. But store up for yourselves treasures in heaven, where moth and rust do not destroy, and where thieves do not break in and steal. For where your treasure is, there your heart will be also. . . .

Wealth and poverty are conditions. The rich and the poor are people. God always focuses on people more than abstractions and concepts. The Scriptures talk more about the rich and the poor than about wealth and poverty. There are some 90 scriptures on the "poor" versus about 16 on "poverty." Why do we tend to focus on abstractions rather than people?

. . . The eye is the lamp of the body. If your eyes are good, your whole body will be full of light. But if your eyes are bad, your whole body will be full of darkness. If then the light within you is darkness, how great is that darkness! No one can serve two masters. Either he will hate the one and love the other, or he will be devoted to the one and despise the other. You cannot serve both God and Money. Therefore I tell you, do not worry about your life, what you will eat or drink; or about your body, what you will wear. Is not life more important than food, and the body more important than clothes? Look at the birds of the air; they do not sow or reap or store away in barns, and yet your heavenly Father feeds them. Are you not much more valuable than they? Who of you by worrying can add a single hour to his life?

And why do you worry about clothes? See how the lilies of the field grow. They do not labor or spin. Yet I tell you that not even Solomon in all his splendor was dressed like one of these. If that is how God clothes the grass of the field, which is here today and tomorrow is thrown into the fire, will he not much more clothe you, O you of little faith? So do not worry, saying, 'What shall we eat?' or 'What shall we drink?' or 'What shall we wear?' For the pagans run after all these things, and your heavenly Father knows that you need them. But seek first his kingdom and his righteousness, and all these things will be given to you as well. Therefore do not worry about tomorrow, for tomorrow will worry about itself. Each day has enough trouble of its own.

2 CORINTHIANS 8:9

For you know the grace of our Lord Jesus Christ, that though he was rich, yet for your sakes he became poor, so that you through his poverty might become rich.

. . . whether economists know it or not, the ideas of wealth and capital that they champion are arguably more spiritual than material. And likewise, whether religious figures know it or not, their tendency to look at the world's poor and see only gloom and doom shows them to be beholden to ideas about wealth and capital that are far more materialistic than spiritual.
William McGurn

1 TIMOTHY 6:6–8

But godliness with contentment is great gain. For we brought nothing into the world, and we can take nothing out of it. But if we have food and clothing, we will be content with that.

1 TIMOTHY 6:17–19

Command those who are rich in this present world not to be arrogant nor to put their hope in wealth, which is so uncertain, but to put their hope in God, who richly provides us with everything for our enjoyment. Command them to do good, to be rich in good deeds, and to be generous and willing to share. In this way they will lay up treasure for themselves as a firm foundation for the coming age, so that they may take hold of the life that is truly life.

> Modern wealth instills in each one a consciousness of being surrounded by opportunities—for enjoyment, for travel, for personal development, for almost anything that is fancied. But . . . unguided by a sense of destiny, either from within or from society, one does not know which opportunities to use and may have the disquieting feeling either of living arbitrarily or of being strangely immobilized on the very boundaries of happiness. *Glenn Tinder*

HEBREWS 13:5

Keep your lives free from the love of money and be content with what you have, because God has said, "Never will I leave you; never will I forsake you."

JAMES 1:10–11

But the one who is rich should take pride in his low position, because he will pass away like a wild flower. For the sun rises with scorching heat and withers the plant; its blossom falls and its beauty is destroyed. In the same way, the rich man will fade away even while he goes about his business.

1 PETER 4:10

Each of you should use whatever gift you have received to serve others, as faithful stewards of God's grace in its various forms.

16.1 In what ways should our attitude toward wealth differ from the world's view?

16.2 What purpose does wealth have in your life?

16.3 Would you agree that wealth is ultimately the ability and opportunity to lovingly serve and bless others?

16.4 What are you doing to productively grow and deliberately utilize your capital for the sake of the Kingdom?

కం

Our capital, our assets, our wealth must be grown and employed productively. Our responsibility flows out of the "creation mandate" in Genesis 1:27, that we be fruitful and multiply. This mandate is reiterated in many places in the Scriptures.

17. The Scriptures tell us that wealth is not just material; we have other resources that are far more valuable. Note some of the other kinds of wealth available to a follower of Christ.

PSALM 90:12
Teach us to number our days, that we may gain a heart of wisdom.

PROVERBS 3:13-18
Blessed are those who find wisdom, those who gain understanding, for she is more profitable than silver and yields better returns than gold. She is more precious than rubies; nothing you desire can compare with her. Long life is in her right hand; in her left hand are riches and honor. Her ways are pleasant ways, and all her paths are peace. She is a tree of life to those who take hold of her; those who hold her fast will be blessed.

It is not the "treasure" that is in view in the following scripture, but the "treasuring." Christ is concerned here because what we treasure reveals the true condition and structure of our hearts and souls.

MATTHEW 6:19-21
Do not store up for yourselves treasures on earth, where moth and rust destroy, and where thieves break in and steal. But store up for yourselves treasures in heaven, where moth and rust do not destroy, and where thieves do not break in and steal. For where your treasure is, there your heart will be also.

ROMANS 11:33
Oh, the depth of the riches of the wisdom and knowledge of God! How unsearchable his judgments, and his paths beyond tracing out!

EPHESIANS 1:18
I pray also that the eyes of your heart may be enlightened in order that you may know the hope to which he has called you, the riches of his glorious inheritance in the saints . . .

> As the body wears clothes and the bones are covered with skin with our hearts inside, so are we, soul and body, clad in the goodness of God. Our soul is so wonderfully loved of him that no one can comprehend it.
> *Julian of Norwich (1342-?)*

EPHESIANS 2:7
. . . in order that in the coming ages he might show the incomparable riches of his grace, expressed in his kindness to us in Christ Jesus.

EPHESIANS 3:16
I pray that out of his glorious riches he may strengthen you with power through his Spirit in your inner being. . . .

ROMANS 15:5
May the God who gives endurance and encouragement give you the same attitude of mind toward each other that Christ Jesus had . . .

> Jesus, through his death and ressurection, established a new community, which is intended not just to proclaim to all the message of a new relationship with God through Christ, but also to model to the world a truly relational community. *Michael Schluter*

1 CORINTHIANS 13:13
And now these three remain: faith, hope and love. But the greatest of these is love.

REVELATION 3:17–18
You say, 'I am rich; I have acquired wealth and do not need a thing.' But you do not realize that you are wretched, pitiful, poor, blind and naked. I counsel you to buy from me gold refined in the fire, so you can become rich; and white clothes to wear, so you can cover your shameful nakedness; and salve to put on your eyes, so you can see.

17.1 What kinds of wealth do these scriptures present? How does such wealth differ from that which normally preoccupies us?

17.2 What is the most important form of capital that we possess?

⊷

In a society founded on various forms of materialism, in which there can be nothing beyond matter or this temporal life, the idea of a transcendent economy designed and ruled by God is difficult to comprehend. Moreover, as we will see in the next section, to live by the values of God's economy often produces resistance from the world.

SECTION NOTES

SECTION 4
ECONOMIES IN CONFLICT

We have seen that God's economy is founded on justice, righteousness, and love. Within God's economy, material wealth is good, but it is not to be our primary pursuit or source of security—and it presents us with dangers. Rather, the purpose of commerce within the economy of God is people. Work, finances, business development, serving the poor, leaving an inheritance, education—all this is only meaningful in the context of a relationship with God and with one another. God did not design us to be cogs in a production line; he designed us to be working participants in an economy that both expresses and leads to unity with each other and an eternal relationship with God.

It should be immediately clear that anyone who wishes to participate in God's economy will experience daily tension with the world's economies in which we live and work. In general, the world's economies are founded on principles that run counter to God's designs. Some economies are better than others, but usually people are seen as the means to some "higher" goal. As a result, they are often exploited. Many experience this daily in the workplace. Justice and righteousness are often cast aside in order to pursue the idol of material wealth.

The power and influence of the idols of materialism, consumerism, power, and technology are maintained in a global system that the Scriptures call the "world" or this "age." The Greek word for this is *kosmos*. It is not a reference to the natural world or the world of people, but the invisible world of ideas and values and goals that oppose the kingdom of God. It is the antithesis of the kingdom of God. And it surrounds us like the air we breathe. It controls cultures and values. Out of this world come social structures, politics, public values and attitudes, and "the market."

When the market goes beyond the place of economic exchange and becomes the basic organizing principle of society, then it moves into the realm of the *kosmos*. When we begin to base decisions exclusively on what the market wants, we are on the edge of succumbing to the *kosmos*.

So, how does a person who is committed to participating in God's economy survive and flourish within any economic system? The purpose of this section is to address this inevitable tension, both in principle and in practice. The Scriptures provide us with the guidance we need to be, as Jesus said in John 17, in the world but not of the world.

18. Examine what the Scriptures reveal about the tensions we will face in this world. What is at the core of this conflict?

JOHN 8:23

But he continued, "You are from below; I am from above. You are of this world; I am not of this world."

JOHN 15:18-20

If the world hates you, keep in mind that it hated me first. If you belonged to the world, it would love you as its own. As it is, you do not belong to the world, but I have chosen you out of the world. That is why the world hates you. Remember the words I spoke to you: 'No servant is greater than his master.' If they persecuted me, they will persecute you also. If they obeyed my teaching, they will obey yours also.

> Only belatedly are we coming to recognize that economics, far from being an independent discipline, is intimately tied, whether we acknowledge it or not, to the broadest questions of worldview. *D.A. Carson*

JOHN 16:33

I have told you these things, so that in me you may have peace. In this world you will have trouble. But take heart! I have overcome the world.

> In an era that prizes tolerance, affirms diversity, and bends over backwards not to appear judgmental, serious claims to truth sound much like an obscenity—often prompting embarrassed looks, rising blood pressures, and even open hostility. . . . The Christian faith, however, unashamedly claims to be objectively true. *Os Guinness*

JOHN 17:9-21

I pray for them. I am not praying for the world, but for those you have given me, for they are yours. All I have is yours, and all you have is mine. And glory has come to me through them. I will remain in the world no longer, but they are still in the world, and I am coming to you.

Holy Father, protect them by the power of your name—the name you gave me—so that they may be one as we are one. While I was with them, I protected them and kept them safe by that name you gave me. None has been lost except the one doomed to destruction so that Scripture would be fulfilled.

I am coming to you now, but I say these things while I am still in the world, so that they may have the full measure of my joy within them. I have given them your word and the world has hated them, for they are not of the world any more than I am of the world.

My prayer is not that you take them out of the world but that you protect them from the evil one. They are not of the world, even as I am not of it. Sanctify them by the truth; your word is truth. As you sent me into the world, I have sent them into the world. For them I sanctify myself, that they too may be truly sanctified.

My prayer is not for them alone. I pray also for those who will believe in me through their message, that all of them may be one, Father, just as you are in me and I am in you. May they also be in us so that the world may believe that you have sent me.

The problem is that balance between making a living and making a life is becoming harder to pull off because the logic of the new economy dictates that more attention be paid to work and less to personal life. . . . The emerging economy—turbulence and all—is offering unprecedented (economic) opportunities. . . . But what it means for the rest of our lives—the parts that depend on firm relationships, continuity, and stability—is acutely problematic. *Former Secretary of Labor Robert Reich*

ROMANS 12:1–2
Therefore, I urge you, brothers, in view of God's mercy, to offer your bodies as living sacrifices, holy and pleasing to God—this is your spiritual act of worship. Do not conform any longer to the pattern of this world, but be transformed by the renewing of your mind. Then you will be able to test and approve what God's will is—his good, pleasing and perfect will.

This principle of living with tension has always been important, but it is magnified under the conditions of modernity. If modernity represents a massive shift of the accent from the spiritual to the secular, we must consciously become deeper and more spiritual even as modernity makes us ever more knowledgeable and skilled on the secular level. *Os Guinness*

1 CORINTHIANS 1:20
Where is the wise man? Where is the scholar? Where is the philosopher of this age? Has not God made foolish the wisdom of the world?

1 CORINTHIANS 2:12
We have not received the spirit of the world but the Spirit who is from God, that we may understand what God has freely given us.

Edward Gibbon (1737–1794) in his *Decline and Fall of the Roman Empire* said that the following attributes marked Rome at its end: first, a mounting love of show and luxury (that is, affluence); second, a widening gap between the very rich and the very poor; third, an obsession with sex; fourth, freakishness in the arts, masquerading as originality, and enthusiasms pretending to be creativity; fifth, an increased desire to live off the state. It all sounds so familiar . . . we are back in Rome. *Francis A. Schaeffer*

2 CORINTHIANS 4:4

The god of this age has blinded the minds of unbelievers, so that they cannot see the light of the gospel of the glory of Christ, who is the image of God.

EPHESIANS 2:2

. . . in which you used to live when you followed the ways of this world and of the ruler of the kingdom of the air, the spirit who is now at work in those who are disobedient.

> The problem of leading a Christian life in a non-Christian society is now very present to us. . . . And as for the Christian who is not aware of this dilemma—and he is the majority—he is becoming more and more de-Christianized by all sorts of unconscious pressure: paganism holds the most valuable advertising space. *Nobel Prize winner T.S. Eliot*

EPHESIANS 6:12

For our struggle is not against flesh and blood, but against the rulers, against the authorities, against the powers of this dark world and against the spiritual forces of evil in the heavenly realms.

COLOSSIANS 2:8

See to it that no one takes you captive through hollow and deceptive philosophy, which depends on human tradition and the basic principles of this world rather than on Christ.

2 PETER 1:4

Through these he has given us his very great and precious promises, so that through them you may participate in the divine nature and escape the corruption in the world caused by evil desires.

> Capital markets . . . can function only when people trust the system. A financial system ridden with conflicts of interest, creative accounting, and excessive exuberance is dangerous precisely because it can destroy the public's trust and cause people to pull out their money. *Austan Goolsbee*

1 JOHN 2:15–17

Do not love the world or anything in the world. If anyone loves the world, the love of the Father is not in him. For everything in the world—the cravings of sinful man, the lust of his eyes and the boasting of what he has and does—comes not from the Father but from the world. The world and its desires pass away, but the man who does the will of God lives forever.

1 JOHN 3:13

Do not be surprised, my brothers, if the world hates you.

1 JOHN 4:3–5

. . . but every spirit that does not acknowledge Jesus is not from God. This is the spirit of the antichrist, which you have heard is coming and even now is already in the world. You, dear children, are from God and have overcome them, because the one who is in you is greater than the one who is in the world. They are from the world and therefore speak from the viewpoint of the world, and the world listens to them.

1 JOHN 5:19

We know that we are children of God, and that the whole world is under the control of the evil one.

18.1 Because the world's systems operate on human principles, to live according to God's design in economic affairs may not always be the road to "success." What kind of opposition and difficulties might you expect?

18.2 How does the economy of God conflict with the world's economies?

✎

At the core of the conflict between God's economy and the world's economies is one fundamental question: Are we serving God or something else? That question is at the heart of every decision we make in our professions. The Scriptures demonstrate our propensity to worship many things other than God. It's a centuries-old problem with catastrophic consequences, but it still plagues us today.

Idolatry is destructive because to substitute anything for God is to cut oneself off from life. This is the delusion of idolatry. We come to the idol believing it will give life. Then we discover, often too late, that it leads to spiritual and relational death.

Why should we discuss idolatry in relation to economics rather than behaviors such as greed and selfishness and ambition? Because greed and corruption are symptoms of underlying idolatry. To attempt to change behavior without changing the driving beliefs or dominating allegiances in our lives will be an exercise in futility.

19. Let's first review the pathology of idolatry. What are the fundamental characteristics of idol worship?

EXODUS 20:4

You shall not make for yourself an idol in the form of anything in heaven above or on the earth beneath or in the waters below.

DEUTERONOMY 4:15–19

Therefore watch yourselves very carefully, so that you do not become corrupt and make for yourselves an idol, an image of any shape, whether formed like a man or a woman, or like any animal on earth or any bird that flies in the air, or like any creature that moves along the ground or any fish in the waters below. And when you look up to the sky and see the sun, the moon and the stars—all the heavenly array—do not be enticed into bowing down to them and worshiping things the LORD your God has apportioned to all the nations under heaven.

1 CHRONICLES 16:25–27

For great is the LORD and most worthy of praise; he is to be feared above all gods. For all the gods of the nations are idols, but the LORD made the heavens. Splendor and majesty are before him; strength and joy in his dwelling place.

> Idols will inevitably involve self-centeredness, self-inflation, and self-deception. Idolatry begins with the counterfeiting of God, because only with a counterfeit of God can people remain the center of their lives and loyalties, autonomous architects of their futures. *Richard Keyes*

PSALM 106:35–39

. . . but they mingled with the nations and adopted their customs. They worshiped their idols, which became a snare to them. They sacrificed their sons and their daughters to demons. They shed innocent blood, the blood of their sons and daughters, whom they sacrificed to the idols of Canaan, and the land was desecrated by their blood. They defiled themselves by what they did; by their deeds they prostituted themselves.

PSALM 115:4–8

But their idols are silver and gold, made by the hands of men. They have mouths, but cannot speak, eyes, but they cannot see; they have ears, but cannot hear, noses, but they cannot smell; they have hands, but cannot feel, feet, but they cannot walk; nor can they utter a sound with their throats. Those who make them will be like them, and so will all who trust in them.

HABAKKUK 2:18

Of what value is an idol, since a man has carved it? Or an image that teaches lies? For he who makes it trusts in his own creation; he makes idols that cannot speak.

Humane capitalism also depends on a sound moral culture, for a free market readily caters to the moral choices we make, supplying whatever consumers want—from Bibles to pornography. Only a virtuous citizenry will refuse to manufacture or buy products that are immoral and destructive.
Charles Colson

ROMANS 1:18–23

The wrath of God is being revealed from heaven against all the godlessness and wickedness of men who suppress the truth by their wickedness, since what may be known about God is plain to them, because God has made it plain to them. For since the creation of the world God's invisible qualities—his eternal power and divine nature—have been clearly seen, being understood from what has been made, so that men are without excuse. For although they knew God, they neither glorified him as God nor gave thanks to him, but their thinking became futile and their foolish hearts were darkened. Although they claimed to be wise, they became fools and exchanged the glory of the immortal God for images made to look like mortal man and birds and animals and reptiles.

ROMANS 6:16

Don't you know that when you offer yourselves to someone to obey him as slaves, you are slaves to the one whom you obey—whether you are slaves to sin, which leads to death, or to obedience, which leads to righteousness?

Never have people been more the masters of their environment. Yet never has a people felt more deceived and disappointed. For never has a people expected so much more than the world could offer. *Daniel Boorstin*

1 CORINTHIANS 10:14

Therefore, my dear friends, flee from idolatry.

1 JOHN 5:21

Dear children, keep yourselves from idols.

19.1 We place our trust and confidence in idols. How is idolatry manifested in our society today?

19.2 Do you recognize symptoms of idolatry in your own life?

◆

Perhaps the most pervasive idol of our times is materialism, which states that God does not exist and that there is only matter that came into existence by chance. This worldview is an appealing crutch because it removes our need to surrender to a divine authority. It emboldens us to chart our own course in our own way. Taken to the extreme, materialism means that everything is permissible. The idol of materialism is not new, but over the last 300 years it has found conditions that have reinforced its persuasive power.

20. In the economic realm, materialism is often expressed as the worship of money. Think about the following:

JOB 31:24–28

If I have put my trust in gold or said to pure gold, 'You are my security,' if I have rejoiced over my great wealth, the fortune my hands had gained, if I have regarded the sun in its radiance or the moon moving in splendor, so that my heart was secretly enticed and my hand offered them a kiss of homage, then these also would be sins to be judged, for I would have been unfaithful to God on high.

1 SAMUEL 8:1-3

When Samuel grew old, he appointed his sons as Israel's leaders. The name of his firstborn was Joel and the name of his second was Abijah, and they served at Beersheba. But his sons did not follow his ways. They turned aside after dishonest gain and accepted bribes and perverted justice.

> So too with money-getters: . . . his ailment is not poverty, but insatiability and avarice, arising from the presence in him of a false and unreflecting judgment; and unless someone removes this, like a tapeworm, from his mind, he will never cease to need superfluities—that is, to want what he does not need. *Plutarch (A.D. 46-120)*

PROVERBS 23:4–5

Do not wear yourself out to get rich; have the wisdom to show restraint. Cast but a glance at riches, and they are gone, for they will surely sprout wings and fly off to the sky like an eagle.

ISAIAH 44:12-20

The blacksmith takes a tool and works with it in the coals; he shapes an idol with hammers, he forges it with the might of his arm. He gets hungry and loses his strength; he drinks no water and grows faint. The carpenter measures with a line and makes an outline with a marker; he roughs it out with chisels and marks it with compasses. He shapes it in human form, human form in all its glory, that it may dwell in a shrine. He cut down cedars, or perhaps took a cypress or oak. He let it grow among the trees of the forest, or planted a pine, and the rain made it grow. It is used as fuel for burning; some of it he takes and warms himself, he kindles a fire and bakes bread.

But he also fashions a god and worships it; he makes an idol and bows down to it. Half of the wood he burns in the fire; over it he prepares his meal, he roasts his meat and eats his fill. He also warms himself and says, "Ah! I am warm; I see the fire." From the rest he makes a god, his idol; he bows down to it and worships. He prays to it and says, "Save me! You are my god!"

They know nothing, they understand nothing; their eyes are plastered over so they cannot see, and their minds closed so they cannot understand. No one stops to think, no one has the knowledge or understanding to say, "Half of it I used for fuel; I even baked bread over its coals, I roasted meat and I ate. Shall I make a detestable thing from what is left? Shall I bow down to a block of wood?"

Such a person feeds on ashes; a deluded heart misleads him; he cannot save himself, or say, "Is not this thing in my right hand a lie?"

> There is an aroma of deadness in the subject of our materialism. Our economy, with its focus on the material and the mechanical, embodies an approach to human life with the spirit drained out of it. *Andrew Schmookler*

MATTHEW 6:19–34

Do not store up for yourselves treasures on earth, where moth and rust destroy, and where thieves break in and steal. But store up for yourselves treasures in heaven, where moth and rust do not destroy, and where thieves do not break in and steal. For where your treasure is, there your heart will be also. The eye is the lamp of the body. If your eyes are good, your whole body will be full of light. But if your eyes are bad, your whole body will be full of darkness. If then the light within you is darkness, how great is that darkness! . . .

> Many Christians unconsciously assume that God measures success by the numbers, that more money means more ministry, which means more success for God's kingdom. So they tend to measure their own success as disciples and servants of the Lord by the size of their ministry. *Joel Carpenter*

. . . No one can serve two masters. Either he will hate the one and love the other, or he will be devoted to the one and despise the other. You cannot serve both God and Money.

Therefore I tell you, do not worry about your life, what you will eat or drink; or about your body, what you will wear. Is not life more important than food, and the body more important than clothes? Look at the birds of the air; they do not sow or reap or store away in barns, and yet your heavenly Father feeds them. Are you not much more valuable than they? Who of you by worrying can add a single hour to his life? . . .

And why do you worry about clothes? See how the lilies of the field grow. They do not labor or spin. Yet I tell you that not even Solomon in all his splendor was dressed like one of these. If that is how God clothes the grass of the field, which is here today and tomorrow is thrown into the fire, will he not much more clothe you, O you of little faith? So do not worry, saying, 'What shall we eat?' or 'What shall we drink?' or 'What shall we wear?' For the pagans run after all these things, and your heavenly Father knows that you need them. But seek first his kingdom and his righteousness, and all these things will be given to you as well. Therefore do not worry about tomorrow, for tomorrow will worry about itself. Each day has enough trouble of its own.

> The interests and comforts of modern life so obsess us and possess us that our Christian allegiance to a kingdom that is not of this world is forgotten.
> *Henry Blamires*

AMOS 8:5

When will the New Moon be over that we may sell grain, and the Sabbath be ended that we may market wheat?

LUKE 18:18-25

A certain ruler asked him, "Good teacher, what must I do to inherit eternal life?"

"Why do you call me good?" Jesus answered. "No one is good—except God alone. You know the commandments: 'You shall not commit adultery, you shall not murder, you shall not steal, you shall not give false testimony, honor your father and mother.'"

"All these I have kept since I was a boy," he said.

When Jesus heard this, he said to him, "You still lack one thing. Sell everything you have and give to the poor, and you will have treasure in heaven. Then come, follow me."

When he heard this, he became very sad, because he was very wealthy. Jesus looked at him and said, "How hard it is for the rich to enter the kingdom of God! Indeed, it is easier for a camel to go through the eye of a needle than for someone who is rich to enter the kingdom of God."

JAMES 5:1-3

Now listen, you rich people, weep and wail because of the misery that is coming upon you. Your wealth has rotted, and moths have eaten your clothes. Your gold and silver are corroded. Their corrosion will testify against you and eat your flesh like fire. You have hoarded wealth in the last days.

20.1 Purpose, value, meaning come from a person, the Creator. If the material is all there is and there is no ultimate purpose except to survive, what impact does this have on our economic life? On

individuals, families, and society? What behavior does this lead to?

20.2 There is always fear involved in worship. It requires us to bow down before the idol. What are the anxieties and fears of a person whose faith and trust is in material wealth? Which of these do you experience?

20.3 How do you resolve the tension of dealing with material things while not placing your confidence in them?

21. Our thesis is that all idols promise life but leave us with enslaved and meaningless lives. This is also true when the idol is money. What are some warnings about money as an idol in the Scriptures?

PROVERBS 11:28
> Whoever trusts in his riches will fall, but the righteous will thrive like a green leaf.

> Through the centuries idols have changed their shape, but they have not disappeared or lost their seductiveness. . . . States and parties, money and material possessions, are finite and man-made and are far more alluring objects of worship, at least for modern peoples, than are images of animals and other creatures. *Glenn Tinder*

PROVERBS 23:4–5
> Do not wear yourself out to get rich; have the wisdom to show restraint. Cast but a glance at riches, and they are gone, for they will surely sprout wings and fly off to the sky like an eagle.

PROVERBS 27:24
> . . . for riches do not endure forever, and a crown is not secure for all generations.

> The more highly industrialized the country, the more easily a materialistic philosophy will flourish in it, and the more deadly that philosophy will be. . . . And the tendency of unlimited industrialism is to create bodies of men and women—of all classes—detached from tradition, alienated from religion and susceptible to mass suggestion: in other words, a mob. And a mob will be no less a mob if it is well-fed, well-clothed, well-housed and well-disciplined.
> *T.S. Eliot*

PROVERBS 28:6

Better a poor man whose walk is blameless than a rich man whose ways are perverse.

PROVERBS 28:11

A rich man may be wise in his own eyes, but a poor man who has discernment sees through him.

PROVERBS 30:7–9

Two things I ask of you, O LORD; do not refuse me before I die: Keep falsehood and lies far from me; give me neither poverty nor riches, but give me only my daily bread. Otherwise, I may have too much and disown you and say, 'Who is the LORD?' Or I may become poor and steal, and so dishonor the name of my God.

> The chief advantage (of inflationary policies) . . . for the government is that it may pay its debts and further the ambitions of its leaders by means of a printing press. . . . That is the alchemist's trick of creating something of value without work. Whether the wizard mutters incantations, mixes formulas, or runs printing presses, he attempts to produce bread without bothering to plow, sow, reap, grind, and bake. He tries to create value ex nihilo and imitate the creative power of God. *Herbert Schlossberg*

ECCLESIASTES 5:10

Whoever loves money never has money enough; whoever loves wealth is never satisfied with his income. This too is meaningless.

MARK 8:36

What good is it for a man to gain the whole world, yet forfeit his soul?

> At the apex of any theological system, of course, is its doctrine of God. In the new theology this celestial pinnacle is occupied by The Market, which I capitalize to signify both the mystery that enshrouds it and the reverence it inspires in business folk. *Harvey Cox*

MARK 10:21–23

Jesus looked at him and loved him. "One thing you lack," he said. "Go, sell everything you have and give to the poor, and you will have treasure in heaven. Then come, follow me."

At this the man's face fell. He went away sad, because he had great wealth. Jesus looked around and said to his disciples, "How hard it is for the rich to enter the kingdom of God!"

LUKE 8:14

The seed that fell among thorns stands for those who hear, but as they go on their way they are choked by life's worries, riches and pleasures, and they do not mature.

> In the chapel of The Market, . . . the First Commandment is 'There is never enough.' *Harvey Cox*

LUKE 12:32-34

Do not be afraid, little flock, for your Father has been pleased to give you the kingdom. Sell your possessions and give to the poor. Provide purses for yourselves that will not wear out, a treasure in heaven that will not be exhaused, where no thief comes near and no moth destroys. For where your treasure is, there you heart will be also.

1 TIMOTHY 6:9-10

People who want to get rich fall into temptation and a trap and into many foolish and harmful desires that plunge men into ruin and destruction. For the love of money is a root of all kinds of evil. Some people, eager for money, have wandered from the faith and pierced themselves with many griefs.

21.1 What is a healthy perspective on wealth?

21.2 What deceptions lead to money becoming an idol? Why do such lies have power over us?

21.3 Why is financial success so often detrimental to spiritual health?

๛

Materialism is the "parent" of several sub-idols that pervade our society. One of the most common today is the idol of consumerism. Consumerism leads us to define ourselves by what we have. We live in an economy that is based on creating consumer desires. It is assumed that economic progress requires a consumer society. Therefore, we build rituals out of buying and selling. We create holidays for this purpose. We build in obsolescence. Last year's model is soon passé. We demand more choices.

22. Consumerism's lie functions by making us believe that our desires are actually needs. Products are marketed to deceive us into thinking that they will revolutionize our lives. For example, in order to be content we "need" a new car. What do the following scriptures say about the "wants" of people?

GENESIS 3:2-8

The woman said to the serpent, "We may eat fruit from the trees in the garden, but God did say, 'You must not eat fruit from the tree that is in the middle of the garden, and you must not touch it, or you will die.'" "You will not certainly die," the serpent said to the woman. "For God knows that when you eat from it your eyes will be opened, and you will be like God, knowing good and evil." When the woman saw that the fruit of the tree was good for food and pleasing to the eye, and also desirable for gaining wisdom, she took some and ate it. She also gave some to her husband, who was with her, and he ate it. Then the eyes of both of them were opened, and they realized they were naked; so they sewed fig leaves together and made coverings for themselves. Then the man and his wife heard the sound of the Lord God as he was walking in the garden in the cool of the day, and they hid from the Lord God among the trees of the garden.

> In theory, freedom has come to mean little more than doing and saying what we please. In practice, it has been reduced for many to picking among the trivial alternatives offered in the capitalist marketplace. *Glenn Tinder*

PROVERBS 13:25

The righteous eat to their hearts' content, but the stomach of the wicked goes hungry.

PROVERBS 27:20

Death and Destruction are never satisfied, and neither are the eyes of man.

> Insatiability itself is as old as humanity, or at least the fall of humanity. Unique to modern capitalism and consumerism are the idealization and constant encouragement of insatiability—the deification of dissatisfaction. *Rodney Clapp*

ECCLESIASTES 4:8

There was a man all alone; he had neither son nor brother. There was no end to his toil, yet his eyes were not content with his wealth. "For whom am I toiling," he asked, "and why am I depriving myself of enjoyment?" This too is meaningless—a miserable business!

ECCLESIASTES 5:10

Whoever loves money never has money enough; whoever loves wealth is never satisfied with his income. This too is meaningless.
banquets, tambourines and flutes and wine, but they have no regard for the deeds of the LORD, no respect for the work of his hands.

ECCLESIASTES 6:3

A man may have a hundred children and live many years; yet no matter how long he lives, if he cannot enjoy his prosperity and does not receive proper burial, I say that a stillborn child is better off than he.

All true needs—such as food, drink, and companionship—are satiable. Illegitimate wants—pride, envy, greed—are insatiable. By their nature they cannot be satisfied. In that sense materialism is the opium of the people. Enough is never enough. *Herbert Schlossberg*

ECCLESIASTES 6:7

All man's efforts are for his mouth, yet his appetite is never satisfied.

We can't turn life into a pleasure. But we can choose such pleasures as are worthy of us and our immortal souls. *G.K. Chesterton*

ISAIAH 5:7-12

The vineyard of the LORD Almighty is the house of Israel, and the men of Judah are the garden of his delight. And he looked for justice, but saw bloodshed; for righteousness, but heard cries of distress. Woe to you who add house to house and join field to field till no space is left and you live alone in the land.

The LORD Almighty has declared in my hearing: "Surely the great houses will become desolate, the fine mansions left without occupants. A ten-acre ineyard will produce only a bath of wine, a homer of seed only an ephah of grain."

Woe to those who rise early in the morning to run after their drinks, who stay up late at night till they are inflamed with wine. They have harps and lyres at their banquets, tambourines and flutes and wine, but they have no regard for the deeds of the Lord, no respect for the work of his hands.

1 TIMOTHY 6:6-10

But godliness with contentment is great gain. For we brought nothing into the world, and we can take nothing out of it. But if we have food and clothing, we will be content with that. Those who want to get rich fall into temptation and a trap and into many foolish and harmful desires that plunge people into ruin and destruction. For the love of money is a root of all kinds of evil. Some people, eager for money, have wandered from the faith and pierced themselves with many griefs.

1 JOHN 2:15-17
    Do not love the world or anything in the world. If anyone loves the world, love for the Father is not in them. For everything in the world—the lust of the flesh, the lust of the eyes, and the pride of life—comes not from the Father but from the world. The world and its desires pass away, but whoever does the will of God lives forever.

22.1 What creates "wants"?

22.2 What are the anxieties and fears of the consumerist? To what destructive behaviors could this lead?

22.3 How can we make distinctions between our needs and wants?

22.4 Is it wrong to desire unnecessary material things?

23. Analyze the destructive consequences of a consumerist from the following:

PROVERBS 21:17
    He who loves pleasure will become poor; whoever loves wine and oil will never be rich.

> Almost all our modern philosophies have been devised to convince us that the good of man is to be found on this earth. . . . They begin by trying to persuade you that earth can be made into a heaven . . . *C.S. Lewis*

PROVERBS 22:7
    The rich rule over the poor, and the borrower is servant to the lender.

LUKE 12:15–21
    Then he said to them, "Watch out! Be on your guard against all kinds of greed; a man's life does not consist in the abundance of his possessions."

And he told them this parable: "The ground of a certain rich man produced a good crop. He thought to himself, 'What shall I do? I have no place to store my crops.' Then he said, 'This is what I'll do. I will tear down my barns and build bigger ones, and there I will store all my grain and my goods. And I'll say to myself, 'You have plenty of good things laid up for many years. Take life easy; eat, drink and be merry.'

"But God said to him, 'You fool! This very night your life will be demanded from you. Then who will get what you have prepared for yourself?'"

This is how it will be with anyone who stores up things for himself but is not rich toward God.

PROVERBS 25:16, 27-28

If you find honey, eat just enough— too much of it, and you will vomit. . . . It is not good to eat too much honey, nor is it honorable to search out matters that are too deep. Like a city whose walls are broken through is a person who lacks self-control.

> If we consider the unblushing promises of reward and the staggering nature of the rewards promised in the Gospels, it would seem that our Lord finds our desires not too strong, but too weak. We are half-hearted creatures, fooling about with drink and sex and ambition when infinite joy is offered us, like an ignorant child who wants to go on making mud pies in a slum because he cannot imagine what is meant by the offer of a holiday at the sea. We are far too easily pleased. *C.S. Lewis*

ROMANS 16:18

For such people are not serving our Lord Christ, but their own appetites. By smooth talk and flattery they deceive the minds of naive people.

PHILIPPIANS 3:18–19

For, as I have often told you before and now say again even with tears, many live as enemies of the cross of Christ. Their destiny is destruction, their god is their stomach, and their glory is in their shame. Their mind is on earthly things.

23.1 Much of current consumerism is fueled by debt. What is the effect of such debt on your life? Your capital?

23.2 What emotional consequences might the illusions and false promises of consumerism produce in people?

24. Ultimately, a consumerist lifestyle points to a misdirected attempt to quench a legitimate hunger and thirst, the real desire of our lives. What is that?

PSALM 42:1–2

As the deer pants for streams of water, so my soul pants for you, O God. My soul thirsts for God, for the living God. When can I go and meet with God?

> Practicing the religion of consumerism is like drinking salt water: The more you drink, the thirstier you get. *Charles Colson*

PSALM 63:1

O God, you are my God, earnestly I seek you; my soul thirsts for you, my body longs for you, in a dry and weary land where there is no water.

PSALM 63:5

My soul will be satisfied as with the richest of foods; with singing lips my mouth will praise you.

PSALM 103:5

. . . who satisfies your desires with good things so that your youth is renewed like the eagle's.

PSALM 107:9

. . . for he satisfies the thirsty and fills the hungry with good things.

ISAIAH 58:10–11

. . . and if you spend yourselves in behalf of the hungry and satisfy the needs of the oppressed, then your light will rise in the darkness, and your night will become like the noonday. The LORD will guide you always; he will satisfy your needs in a sun-scorched land and will strengthen your frame. You will be like a well-watered garden, like a spring whose waters never fail.

24.1 Consumerism is much like an addiction to junk food that can mask a real need for true nutrition. How do we acquire and develop a hunger and taste for "real food"?

24.2 How will being satisfied this way enable us to better conduct our economic affairs?

❧

Because the world's values and principles saturate our lives, we risk falling into a trap called "syncretism." The Christian worldview becomes blended with other ideas. What is deemed "normal" in society—no matter how immoral or unwise—seems normal to us. Unethical business practices begin to seem like standard procedure. In short, our idols impact our lives without us being able to recognize them as being idols. For this reason, it is crucial that we sustain deep engagement with the Scriptures. We need God's word as the reference point for truth in our lives.

25. Each day we are faced with temptations and deceptions as we seek to live according to God's purposes in a corrupt system. In the following scriptures, notice how each decision is infused with moral choices. As you consider your role in God's economy, what are the benefits of choosing God's ways?

PSALM 1

Blessed is the one who does not walk in step with the wicked or stand in the way that sinners take or sit in the company of mockers, but whose delight is in the law of the Lord, and who meditates on his law day and night. That person is like a tree planted by streams of water, which yields its fruit in season and whose leaf does not wither—whatever they do prospers. Not so the wicked! They are like chaff that the wind blows away. Therefore the wicked will not stand in the judgment, nor sinners in the assembly of the righteous. For the Lord watches over the way of the righteous, but the way of the wicked leads to destruction.

JEREMIAH 17:5-8

This is what the Lord says: "Cursed is the one who trusts in man, who draws strength from mere flesh and whose heart turns away from the Lord. That person will be like a bush in the wastelands; they will not see prosperity when it comes. They will dwell in the parched places of the desert, in a salt land where no one lives. But blessed is the one who trusts in the Lord, whose confidence is in him. They will be like a tree planted by the water that sends out its roots by the stream. It does not fear when heat comes; its leaves are always green. It has no worries in a year of drought and never fails to bear fruit."

> More of us today are more anonymous in more situations than any generation in human history. Humanly anonymous and invisible, we must consciously hold ourselves responsible to the one audience—the Audience of One—or succumb to irresponsibility. *Os Guinness*

GALATIANS 5:22-25

But the fruit of the Spirit is love, joy, peace, forbearance, kindness, goodness, faithfulness, gentleness and self-control. Against such things there is no law. Those who belong to Christ Jesus have crucified the flesh with its passions and desires. Since we live by the Spirit, let us keep in step with the Spirit.

> What I did was what everyone should do. If everyone did this Brazil would be a better place. And there's nothing better in life than to come home and sleep with a clear conscience. . . . This is all I want for my family and me.
> *Francisco Cavalcante, a Brazilian airport janitor responding to questions about why he returned a lost travel bag containing $10,000 to its owner.*

2 PETER 1:4

Through these he has given us his very great and precious promises, so that through them you may participate in the divine nature, having escaped the corruption in the world caused by evil desires.

ISAIAH 33:15

Those who walk righteously and speak what is right, who reject gain from extortion and keep their hands from accepting bribes, who stop their ears against plots of murder and shut their eyes against contemplating evil— they are the ones who will dwell on the heights, whose refuge will be the mountain fortress. Their bread will be supplied, and water will not fail them.

25.1 In light of the temptations we have studied, how do these scriptures help us keep in step with the Spirit?

25.2 Doing what is right in the context of a corrupt economic system often leads to financial loss. How do we live according to the Scriptures in the face of such trials?

~§

Our own daily anxieties and fears reveal the idols to which we are subordinated. These must be replaced by a fear of God and surrender to His ways. We will face tremendous struggle in our attempt to throw off the shackles of idolatry and the world system. However, God gives us powerful resources with which to do so. One person at a time, one household at a time, we can take back lost ground. We cannot escape the struggle, but we can stand firm in it.

In the next section, we will unwrap what the Scriptures reveal about a revolutionary way of living, one that is fully aligned with a generous God.

Section Notes

SECTION 5
LIVING GENEROUSLY

What God created, he gave to people (Genesis 1). "The heavens belong to the Lord, but the Earth he has given to mankind" (Psalm 115:16). God's economy is founded on God's generosity. All of life begins with a gift. Think of it! If we accept God as our model for life, could it be that giving rather than receiving, creating rather than consuming, generosity rather than greed should be at the heart of all economic activity?

26. Examine this theme as it develops across the spectrum of the Scriptures.

GENESIS 12:2 (GOD TO ABRAHAM)

I will make you into a great nation and I will bless you; I will make your name great, and you will be a blessing.

GENESIS 26:3–4

Stay in this land for a while, and I will be with you and will bless you. For to you and your descendants I will give all these lands and will confirm the oath I swore to your father Abraham. I will make your descendants as numerous as the stars in the sky and will give them all these lands, and through your offspring all nations on earth will be blessed. . . .

> Giving reflects not only love but also faith. It looks to God as the source of all that we possess. Therefore, it believes that gifts can be given and that resources don't need to be hoarded.

PSALM 37:25–26

I was young and now I am old, yet I have never seen the righteous forsaken or their children begging bread. They are always generous and lend freely; their children will be blessed.

PSALM 104:27–28

These all look to you to give them their food at the proper time. When you give it to them, they gather it up; when you open your hand, they are satisfied with good things.

PSALM 111:4-5

He has caused his wonders to be remembered; the Lord is gracious and compassionate. He provides food for those who fear him; he remembers his covenant forever.

> Generosity can be multiplied by the creative use of the abilities God has given us. We can not only multiply the amount we give, but we can increase the effectiveness of what we give, devising ways to make our generosity even more beneficial. *Jake Barnett*

PROVERBS 3:27-28

Do not withhold good from those who deserve it, when it is in your power to act. Do not say to your neighbor, "Come back later; I'll give it tomorrow"—when you now have it with you.

PROVERBS 21:26

All day long he craves for more, but the righteous give without sparing.

PROVERBS 28:27

He who gives to the poor will lack nothing, but he who closes his eyes to them receives many curses.

JEREMIAH 29:7 (TO THE EXILES OF JUDAH)

Also, seek the peace and prosperity of the city to which I have carried you into exile. Pray to the LORD for it, because if it prospers, you too will prosper.

JOHN 3:16

For God so loved the world that he gave his one and only Son, that whoever believes in him shall not perish but have eternal life.

> George Gilder, in writing about the role of generosity in creating economic health, says, ". . . the heart of the system must always be giving, not taking, or the body (the economic system) will run down and rot."

ACTS 20:33-35

I have not coveted anyone's silver or gold or clothing. You yourselves know that these hands of mine have supplied my own needs and the needs of my companions. In everything I did, I showed you that by this kind of hard work we must help the weak, remembering the words the Lord Jesus himself said: 'It is more blessed to give than to receive.'

Give up yourself, and you will find your real self. Lose your life and you will save it. . . . Keep back nothing. Nothing that you have not given away will be really yours. Nothing in you that has not died will ever be raised from the dead. Look for yourself, and you will find in the long run only hatred, loneliness, despair, rage, ruin, and decay. But look for Christ and you will find him, and with him everything else thrown in. *C.S. Lewis*

ROMANS 8:32

He who did not spare his own Son, but gave him up for us all—how will he not also, along with him, graciously give us all things?

PHILIPPIANS 2:4-7

Each of you should look not only to your own interests, but also to the interests of others. Your attitude should be the same as that of Christ Jesus: Who, being in very nature God . . . made himself nothing.

2 CORINTHIANS 8:9

For you know the grace of our Lord Jesus Christ, that though he was rich, yet for your sakes he became poor, so that you through his poverty might become rich.

For most of us, learning to give . . . takes discipline at first because it runs contrary to our natural selfishness. It takes very little practice, however, for the experience of giving to stimulate our hearts' generosity that comes from God's image within us. When this happens, giving becomes a privilege—one of the most satisfying of all spiritual experiences. *Jake Barnett*

GALATIANS 5:13

You, my brothers, were called to be free. But do not use your freedom to indulge the sinful nature; rather, serve one another in love.

EPHESIANS 4:28

He who has been stealing must steal no longer, but must work, doing something useful with his own hands, that he may have something to share with those in need.

26.1 What if giving rather than getting characterized the moral heart of an economy? How would this impact the economic and social challenges of our world?

26.2 How can generosity be a foundational virtue of your life?

27. We are designed in the image of relational God. He expects us to participate meaningfully with one another. In the economy of God, generosity is foundational for community life.

ROMANS 12:13
Share with God's people who are in need. Practice hospitality.

1 CORINTHIANS 12:25-26
. . . there should be no division in the body, but that its parts should have equal concern for each other. If one part suffers, every part suffers with it; if one part is honored, every part rejoices with it.

> In genuine community, the individual as the giver is deemphasized while the concept of a community of sharers is emphasized. In true community, giving becomes sharing. *Jake Barnett*

2 CORINTHIANS 8:14
At the present time your plenty will supply what they need, so that in turn their plenty will supply what you need. Then there will be equality.

ACTS 4:32
All the believers were one in heart and mind. No one claimed that any of his possession was his own, but they shared everything they had.

27.1 What has been your experience with giving in the context of a community?

27.2 What barriers to this kind of giving do you notice in our culture?

28. Read the following passages and identify what God wants from us when we give.

2 CORINTHIANS 8:12
For if the willingness is there, the gift is acceptable according to what one has, not according to what he does not have.

MARK 12:42
But a poor widow came and put in two very small copper coins, worth only a fraction of a penny. Calling his disciples to him, Jesus said, "I tell you the truth, this

poor widow has put more into the treasury than all the others. They all gave out of their wealth; but she, out of her poverty, put in everything—all she had to live on.

MARK 14:3-7

While he was in Bethany, reclining at the table in the home of a man known as Simon the Leper, a woman came with an alabaster jar of very expensive perfume, made of pure nard. She broke the jar and poured the perfume on his head. Some of those present were saying indignantly to one another, "Why this waste of perfume? It could have been sold for more than a year's wages and the money given to the poor." And they rebuked her harshly.

"Leave her alone," said Jesus. "Why are you bothering her? She has done a beautiful thing to me. The poor you will always have with you, and you can help them any time you want. But you will not always have me. She did what she could. She poured perfume on my body beforehand to prepare for my burial. I tell you the truth, wherever the gospel is preached throughout the world, what she has done will also be told, in memory of her."

MATTHEW 25:34-46

Then the King will say to those on his right, 'Come, you who are blessed by my Father; take your inheritance, the kingdom prepared for you since the creation of the world. For I was hungry and you gave me something to eat, I was thirsty and you gave me something to drink, I was a stranger and you invited me in, I needed clothes and you clothed me, I was sick and you looked after me, I was in prison and you came to visit me.'

Then the righteous will answer him, 'Lord, when did we see you hungry and feed you, or thirsty and give you something to drink? When did we see you a stranger and invite you in, or needing clothes and clothe you? When did we see you sick or in prison and go to visit you?'

The King will reply, 'Truly I tell you, whatever you did for one of the least of these brothers and sisters of mine, you did for me.'

Then he will say to those on his left, 'Depart from me, you who are cursed, into the eternal fire prepared for the devil and his angels. For I was hungry and you gave me nothing to eat, I was thirsty and you gave me nothing to drink, I was a stranger and you did not invite me in, I needed clothes and you did not clothe me, I was sick and in prison and you did not look after me.'

They also will answer, 'Lord, when did we see you hungry or thirsty or a stranger or needing clothes or sick or in prison, and did not help you?'

He will reply, 'Truly I tell you, whatever you did not do for one of the least of these, you did not do for me.' Then they will go away to eternal punishment, but the righteous to eternal life.

The king gives us a powerful illustration of the economy of God in action. The economy of God is the economy of the kingdom of God. The scripture in Matthew 25 reflects God's economy through our engagement with those in need. His economy is about people.

PHILIPPIANS 4:15-17

Moreover, as you Philippians know, in the early days of your acquaintance with the gospel, when I set out from Macedonia, not one church shared with me in the matter of giving and receiving, except you only; for even when I was in Thessalonica, you sent me aid more than once when I was in need. Not that I desire your gifts; what I desire is that more be credited to your account.

2 CORINTHIANS 9:7

Each of you should give what you have decided in your heart to give, not reluctantly or under compulsion, for God loves a cheerful giver.

ACTS 11:29

The disciples, as each one was able, decided to provide help for the brothers and sisters living in Judea.

1 CORINTHIANS 4:7-8

For who makes you different from anyone else? What do you have that you did not receive? And if you did receive it, why do you boast as though you did not. Already you have all you want! Already you have become rich! You have become kings—and that without us!

2 CORINTHIANS 8:3-4

For I testify that they gave as much as they were able, and even beyond their ability. Entirely on their own, they urgently pleaded with us for the privilege of sharing in this service to the Lord's people.

28.1 What do you think is your responsibility to care for those who are "the least" among you?

28.2 What criteria do you use to decide what you give in relation to what you keep?

28.3 Believers in the first century sometimes gave according to what they were "able" to give, and sometimes "beyond their ability" (2 Corinthians 8:3-4). What does this imply in our lives?

29. God's love for us, and thus our love for God, lie at the heart of God's generous economy. What are some ways in which we are participating or will participate in the rewards of living generously for the sake of others?

PHILIPPIANS 3:8-9

What is more, I consider everything a loss because of the surpassing worth of knowing Christ Jesus my Lord, for whose sake I have lost all things. I consider them garbage, that I may gain Christ and be found in him, not having a righteousness of my own that comes from the law, but that which is through faith in Christ—the righteousness that comes from God on the basis of faith.

ISAIAH 58:10-11

. . . and if you spend yourselves in behalf of the hungry and satisfy the needs of the oppressed, then your light will rise in the darkness, and your night will become like the noonday. The Lord will guide you always; he will satisfy your needs in a sun-scorched land and will strengthen your frame. You will be like a well-watered garden, like a spring whose waters never fail.

ISAIAH 55:1-3

Come, all you who are thirsty, come to the waters; and you who have no money, come, buy and eat. Come, buy wine and milk without money and without cost. Why spend money on what is not bread, and your labor on what does not satisfy? Listen, listen to me, and eat what is good, and you will delight in the richest of fare.

LUKE 6:38

Give, and it will be given to you. A good measure, pressed down, shaken together and running over, will be poured into your lap. For with the measure you use, it will be measured to you.

> Through giving, the sphere of our service and its accompanying reward is expanded far beyond our comprehension. I believe the faithful Christian will be amazed to see the extent of the influence of his or her service in eternity.
> *Jake Barnett*

JOHN 17:20-22

My prayer is not for them alone. I pray also for those who will believe in me through their message, that all of them may be one, Father, just as you are in me and I am in you. May they also be in us so that the world may believe that you have sent me. I have given them the glory that you gave me, that they may be one as we are one.

2 CORINTHIANS 9:8, 11

And God is able to bless you abundantly, so that in all things at all times, having all that you need, you will abound in every good work. . . . You will be enriched in every way so that you can be generous on every occasion, and through us your generosity will result in thanksgiving to God.

> . . . our ethical individualism . . . is linked to an economic individualism that, ironically, knows nothing of the sacredness of the individual. Its only standard is money, and the only thing more sacred than money is more money. What economic individualism destroys and what our kind of religious individualism cannot restore is solidarity, a sense of being members of the same body.
> *Robert N. Bellah*

2 CORINTHIANS 9:6

Remember this: Whoever sows sparingly will also reap sparingly, and whoever sows generously will also reap generously.

PROVERBS 11:25

A generous person will prosper; whoever refreshes others will be refreshed.

PHILIPPIANS 4:11-12

I am not saying this because I am in need, for I have learned to be content whatever the circumstances. I know what it is to be in need, and I know what it is to have plenty. I have learned the secret of being content in any and every situation, whether well fed or hungry, whether living in plenty or in want.

29.1 What is the nature of the rewards described in the Scriptures above? How do they compare to the typical rewards people seek in the world's economies?

29.2 Jesus' reward for his generous death on the cross was people. Does the promise of an eternal and relational reward motivate you? How?

⚜

God's generosity was an expression of his love, which is the essence of his nature. Generosity is life giving to those around us, not just in material ways, but in building bonds of love and intimacy. As we imitate God through generous living, we multiply our lives by giving life and new beginnings to those around us. This generosity starts within the relational context of our household and then expands to our broader circle of friendships. The Scriptures also call us to extend our generosity to future generations!

30. We are made in the image of the Creator: serving, creating, sustaining, blessing. All of us, even if we are not the head of a household, have a circle of friends that we influence. What insights do you get from the following scriptures?

PROVERBS 27:23–27

Be sure you know the condition of your flocks, give careful attention to your herds; for riches do not endure forever, and a crown is not secure for all generations. When the hay is removed and new growth appears and the grass from the hills is gathered in, the lambs will provide you with clothing, and the goats with the price of a field. You will have plenty of goats' milk to feed you and your family and to nourish your servant girls.

> Beneficial utilization of wealth is almost always a function of community. The completely selfish person, the traditional miser, is rare indeed. Man must live in community to express God's image, and the majority of people conduct their economic lives in relationship to some community, at least that of family.
> *Jake Barnett*

PROVERBS 31:10–31

A wife of noble character who can find? She is worth far more than rubies. Her husband has full confidence in her and lacks nothing of value. She brings him good, not harm, all the days of her life. She selects wool and flax and works with eager hands. She is like the merchant ships, bringing her food from afar. She gets up while it is still dark; she provides food for her family and portions for her servant girls. She considers a field and buys it; out of her earnings she plants a vineyard. She sets about her work vigorously; her arms are strong for her tasks. She sees that her trading is profitable, and her lamp does not go out at night. In her hand she holds the distaff and grasps the spindle with her fingers.

She opens her arms to the poor and extends her hands to the needy. When it snows, she has no fear for her household; for all of them are clothed in scarlet. She makes coverings for her bed; she is clothed in fine linen and purple. . . . She makes linen garments and sells them, and supplies the merchants with sashes. She is clothed with strength and dignity; she can laugh at the days to come. She speaks with wisdom, and faithful instruction is on her tongue. She watches over the affairs of her household and does not eat the bread of idleness. Her children arise and call her blessed; her husband also, and he praises her: "Many women do noble things, but you surpass them all."

Charm is deceptive, and beauty is fleeting; but a woman who fears the LORD is to be praised. . . .

2 CORINTHIANS 12:14

Now I am ready to visit you for the third time, and I will not be a burden to you, because what I want is not your possessions but you. After all, children should not have to save up for their parents, but parents for their children.

1 TIMOTHY 5:4

But if a widow has children or grandchildren, these should learn first of all to put their religion into practice by caring for their own family and so repaying their parents and grandparents, for this is pleasing to God.

1 TIMOTHY 5:8

If anyone does not provide for his relatives, and especially for his immediate family, he has denied the faith and is worse than an unbeliever.

30.1 What is the relational context in which you live?

30.2 How can you better utilize the resources God has given you to provide more effectively for your household and relational circle?

∽

We should work not only to provide for today but also to provide for tomorrow. We must have a multigenerational perspective in our responsibilities, even as God does in his.

31. What do you notice about the multigenerational perspective from the following scriptures?

DEUTERONOMY 7:9

Know therefore that the LORD your God is God; he is the faithful God, keeping his covenant of love to a thousand generations of those who love him and keep his commands.

PSALM 25:12–13

Who, then, is the man that fears the LORD? He will instruct him in the way chosen for him. He will spend his days in prosperity, and his descendants will inherit the land.

PSALM 33:11

But the plans of the LORD stand firm forever, the purposes of his heart through all generations.

Without posterity, there are no grand designs. There are no high ambitions. Politics becomes insignificant. Even words like justice lose meaning because everything gets reduced to the narrow qualities of the here and now.
David Brooks

PSALM 78:3-8
. . . what we have heard and known, what our fathers have told us. We will not hide them from their children; we will tell the next generation the praiseworthy deeds of the LORD, his power, and the wonders he has done. He decreed statutes for Jacob and established the law in Israel, which he commanded our forefathers to teach their children, so the next generation would know them, even the children yet to be born, and they in turn would tell their children. Then they would put their trust in God and would not forget his deeds but would keep his commands. They would not be like their forefathers—a stubborn and rebellious generation, whose hearts were not loyal to God, whose spirits were not faithful to him.

His name will ever be specially identified with those exertions which, by the blessing of God, removed from England the guilt of the African slave trade, and prepared the way for the abolition of slavery in every colony of the empire: In the prosecution of these objects, he relied, not in vain, on God.
Epitaph of William Wilberforce (1759-1833), British member of Parliament who successfully led the effort to abolish slavery worldwide

PROVERBS 13:22
A good man leaves an inheritance for his children's children, but a sinner's wealth is stored up for the righteous.

PROVERBS 19:14
Houses and wealth are inherited from parents, but a prudent wife is from the LORD.

And as with other facets of our new lives, we can abandon the community we choose almost instantly and switch to another in pursuit of a better deal. . . . These new communities don't require nearly as much commitment as the old did, nor do they offer the same security. . . . *Robert Reich*

ECCLESIASTES 7:11
Wisdom, like an inheritance, is a good thing and benefits those who see the sun.

31.1 Based on these scriptures, what is the nature of a godly legacy?

31.2 Why is it important to leave a legacy? What is the purpose of a legacy?

31.3 How will you deliberately create a legacy for your household? What can you do now to benefit them in the future?

31.4 List a few obstacles to creating a legacy for families today.

31.5 Describe the legacy you want to pass on—both economic and in other ways—to your children and grandchildren.

⁓

George Gilder, author of *Wealth and Poverty,* writes that "The receipt of a legacy, it turns out, often erodes the qualities of entrepreneurship that are needed to perpetuate it." In fact, most family fortunes are gained, consumed and lost in a three-generation span.

Prominent men in business such as Andrew Carnegie, writing on inheritance, or Warren Buffett of Berkshire Hathaway, and Bill Gates of Microsoft have indicated that they do not intend to leave the bulk of their estate to their children for those reasons. Is the wealth the problem or is there something else lacking?

However, God does not withhold an inheritance because he fears that we can't handle it. He takes the risk of providing the inheritance, but he also works to help us develop faith, wisdom, purpose and mature character. He is more concerned about what we do with our lives than with our inheritance.

As imitators of God, we must pass on a legacy that is more than money. Many try to attach conditions to an inheritance or try to determine who is deserving of the inheritance. In many cases, this is an attempt by the dead to maintain control over the living. And this misses the point.

An inheritance, a legacy, is not an end-of-life issue but a living issue. It is not just about what you prepare to leave behind but whom you prepare to leave behind.

Our responsibility is not just to create an inheritance but also to create worthy heirs. This will take significant involvement in the lives of those in your household. God is constantly at work preparing a people who will live to the praise of His glory. Are you?

32. Our responsibilities also reach out beyond our own household to those who are of the "household of faith" (Galatians 6:10). This "household" or "family of believers" refers to the spiritual family we are adopted into when we become followers of Christ. What are our responsibilities?

ROMANS 15:26

For Macedonia and Achaia were pleased to make a contribution for the poor among the saints in Jerusalem.

> . . . above all it is love that binds its members together into a true unity. Far from being a human possibility, however, it has its origin in God. Only through the Spirit is it poured out into Christians' lives. Far from being merely an attitude towards others, it involves a purposive act of will . . . it expresses itself not in mere feeling or inclination but in concrete acts of service.
> *Robert Banks*

1 CORINTHIANS 12:7

Now to each one the manifestation of the Spirit is given for the common good.

1 CORINTHIANS 12:14-21

Even so the body is not made up of one part but of many. Now if the foot should say, "Because I am not a hand, I do not belong to the body," it would not for that reason stop being part of the body. And if the ear should say, "Because I am not an eye, I do not belong to the body," it would not for that reason stop being part of the body. If the whole body were an eye, where would the sense of hearing be? If the whole body were an ear, where would the sense of smell be? But in fact God has placed the parts in the body, every one of them, just as he wanted them to be. If they were all one part, where would the body be? As it is, there are many parts, but one body. The eye cannot say to the hand, "I don't need you!" And the head cannot say to the feet, "I don't need you!"

GALATIANS 2:10

All they asked was that we should continue to remember the poor, the very thing I was eager to do.

GALATIANS 6:9-10

Let us not become weary in doing good, for at the proper time we will reap a harvest if we do not give up. Therefore, as we have opportunity, let us do good to all people, especially to those who belong to the family of believers.

HEBREWS 10:24–25

And let us consider how we may spur one another on toward love and good deeds. Let us not give up meeting together, as some are in the habit of doing, but let us encourage one another—and all the more as you see the Day approaching.

> On the surface, we like what Jesus taught. We all agree that love is good. Who can argue with that? But if we encounter a situation in which love requires us to do something sacrificial, well, then we squirm.
> *Jim Petersen, Glenn McMahan, David Russ*

JAMES 2:1–6

My brothers, as believers in our glorious Lord Jesus Christ, don't show favoritism. Suppose a man comes into your meeting wearing a gold ring and fine clothes, and a poor man in shabby clothes also comes in. If you show special attention to the man wearing fine clothes and say, "Here's a good seat for you," but say to the poor man, "You stand there" or "Sit on the floor by my feet," have you not discriminated among yourselves and become judges with evil thoughts?

Listen, my dear brothers: Has not God chosen those who are poor in the eyes of the world to be rich in faith and to inherit the kingdom he promised those who love him? But you have insulted the poor. Is it not the rich who are exploiting you? Are they not the ones who are dragging you into court?

JAMES 2:15–17

Suppose a brother or sister is without clothes and daily food. If one of you says to him, "Go, I wish you well; keep warm and well fed," but does nothing about his physical needs, what good is it? In the same way, faith by itself, if it is not accompanied by action, is dead.

1 JOHN 3:16–17

This is how we know what love is: Jesus Christ laid down his life for us. And we ought to lay down our lives for our brothers. If anyone has material possessions and sees his brother in need but has no pity on him, how can the love of God be in him?

32.1 How can you serve and strengthen this larger household?

32.2 In what ways does a strong, loving community serve to protect people financially, spiritually, and physically?

32.3 What has been your experience within a community?

&

We finish this study where we began: with the nature of God and the implications of being created in his image. The economy of God is designed to help us flourish, giving us the basis for freedom, individual worth, and community. Wealth and commerce need to be integrated with these dimensions of life, and that only happens within the economy of God.

33. How are the concepts of the freedom and worth of the individual and of the need to be in community with others expressed in the following?

GENESIS 1:26–28

Then God said, "Let us make man in our image, in our likeness, and let them rule over the fish of the sea and the birds of the air, over the livestock, over all the earth, and over all the creatures that move along the ground."

So God created man in his own image, in the image of God he created him; male and female he created them.

God blessed them and said to them, "Be fruitful and increase in number; fill the earth and subdue it. Rule over the fish of the sea and the birds of the air and over every living creature that moves on the ground."

GENESIS 2:18

The LORD God said, "It is not good for the man to be alone. I will make a helper suitable for him."

Because every person was created by a personal God and is not the result of an impersonal cosmic accident, humans have the basis for their intrinsic and infinite value. . . . Without this transcendent basis for human dignity, society easily falls prey to neglecting its weakest members in exchange for expedient goals. *Jim Petersen, Glenn McMahan, David Russ*

DEUTERONOMY 12:8

You are not to do as we do here today, everyone as he sees fit. . . .

JUDGES 21:25

In those days Israel had no king; everyone did as he saw fit.

God, the Father, did His work in collaborative community with other members of the Godhead. What does this say about the need for others in the creative process?

EPHESIANS 4:15–16

... speaking the truth in love, we will in all things grow up into him who is the Head, that is, Christ. From him the whole body, joined and held together by every supporting ligament, grows and builds itself up in love, as each part does its work.

> We who have been embraced by the outstretched arms of the crucified God open our arms even for the enemies—to make space in ourselves for them and invite them in—so that together we may rejoice in the eternal embrace of the triune God. *Miroslav Volf*

HEBREWS 10:24–25

And let us consider how we may spur one another on toward love and good deeds. Let us not give up meeting together, as some are in the habit of doing, but let us encourage one another—and all the more as you see the Day approaching.

33.1 What happens when individual freedoms are allowed to overshadow the needs of others?

33.2 What happens when individual needs are totally subordinated to those of the community?

33.3 Why do these twin truths—the freedom and worth of each person and the need for community—need to be integrated for people to flourish relationally and financially?

33.4 How can we involve our families within an economic community?

✥

Creativity. A wisdom that upholds and enhances life. A fruitful, productive abundance of resources. Astonishing generosity. Freedom. The worth of every person. The indispensability of community. A love that serves others. These are all foundational characteristics, which are at the core of an economic life that reflects God's character and purposes. As God's image bearers, do we exhibit these qualities in our economic lives?

The kingdom of God, as we have seen, includes people in diverse cultures and situations. Our review of wealth and poverty within the economy of God demonstrates that there are economic differences among his people. However, God makes provision for people in all economic situations. A relationship with Christ changes one's status, now and in eternity. The economy of God provides us with dignity, hope, justice, community.

As we represent God's economy through our professional and financial decisions, people experience the presence of God and his goodness. Imagine the transformative effect of working in companies that practice these qualities. Imagine families that exhibit these attributes. Imagine living in a society where the economy is built on the foundations of God's kingdom.

In what ways could you and your family grow in these qualities?

In what ways could your business grow in these qualities?

SECTION NOTES

Taking Action

As we stated at the beginning of this book, the *Scriptural Roots of Commerce* is not designed to only be about the intellect. A true adventure with God, one in which we participate in God's purposes, requires us to put his counsel and designs into practice in every arena. We are called to integrate our professions with God's purposes. God wants us to live, not just learn. We need to begin taking tangible steps toward applying—at work and at home—what he is teaching us.

This is rarely accomplished alone. If you have studied this book with a group of friends, you have an opportunity to think together about how to apply the truths you've discovered so far. A suggestion is to choose one or two principles from this study that most impacted you. Then talk as a group about how you might live out those principles in the context of your work, family, and community. Hopefully, this group of friends can be an ongoing source of encouragement and growth for one another.

The following questions might help guide you in this process.

1. Review this study, including your personal notes, and identify several principles or truths that most impacted your mind and heart. What are these principles and why are they important to you?

2. Looking at your situation and context, what needs to take place in order for you to begin to live differently? What obstacles and risks do you encounter as you contemplate making changes in your work and family?

3. Thinking beyond your personal needs, what can you do to improve the lives of those around you? What needs do you see in your profession and workplace? Think about how to apply these principles in your work, within your broader sphere of influence. Be creative and innovative.

4. Participate with your friends to seek an adventure with God together. What are you learning together from your experiences? The writer of Hebrews wrote: "And let us consider how we may spur one another on toward love and good deeds, not giving up meeting together . . . ." Be committed to one another for the long-term, encouraging each other to innovate ways of doing good through your work and professions.

Bibliography of Works Cited

Aquinas, Thomas. *Summa Theologiae II-II, 66, 2* quoted in *Economic Thinking for the Theologically Minded,* by Samuel Gregg, (University Press of America, 2001), p. 71.

Banks, Robert. *Paul's Idea of Community,* (Hendrickson, 1994), p. 54.

Barclay, William. *The Gospel of Matthew in the Daily Study Bible Series,* (Westminster Press, 1975), p. 323.

Barrett and Johnson. *Our Globe,* 1990; *The Reality of Aid,* 1996.

Barnett, Jake. *Wealth and Wisdom,* (Global Commerce Network, 2015), p. 175, 179, 204.

Behe, Michael. *The Edge of Evolution: The Search for the Limits of Evolution,* (Free Press, 2007), p. 214.

Bellah, Robert. "Religion and the Shape of National Culture," quoted in *The Best of Christian Writing 2000,* John Wilson, editor, (HarperSanFrancisco, 2000), p. 73-74.

Black, Adam and Charles. *Black's Bible Dictionary,* 1954, p. 693.

Blamires, Henry. *Where Do We Stand?,* (Servant Books, 1980), p. 112.

Blomberg, Craig. *Neither Poverty Nor Riches,* (Eerdmans, 1999), p. 19, 41.

Boorstin, Daniel. *The Image,* (Antheneum, 1961), p. 15-16.

Bork, Robert. *On Mars Hill Tape 24,* November/December 1996.

Brooks, David. "The Power of Posterity," *The New York Times,* July 28, 2009, accessed online at http://www.nytimes.com/2009/07/28/opinion/28brooks

Buechner, Frederick. *The Longing for Home,* (HarperSanFrancisco, 1996), p. 13, 158

Bussard, Allan et al. *Code of Ethics and Social Audit: A Manual,* (The Integra Venture), 2002, p. 5.

Carpenter, Joel. Quoted in *Total Truth: Liberating Christianity from its Cultural Captivity,* (Crossway Books, 2005), p. 367.

Carson, D.A. *The Gagging of God,* (Zondervan, 1996), p. 400.

Cavalcante, Francisco. Quoted in *More Than Me,* by Jim Petersen, Glenn McMahan, and David Russ, (NavPress, 2008), p. 75.

Clapp, Rodney (editor). *The Consuming Passion,* (InterVarsity Press, 1998), pages 188, 203.

Chesterton, G.K. *Preface to Pickwick Papers,* by Charles Dickens.

Chrysostom, St. John. Quoted in *Doing Well and Doing Good,* by Os Guinness, (NavPress, 2001), p. 38, 50, 56.

Colson, Charles. *How Now Shall We Live,* (Tyndale, 1999), p. 230, 383, 385, 390.

Coward, Alexander. published email to his students during a university labor strike, accessed online at http://alumni.berkeley.edu/california-magazine/just-in/2013-11-21/cal-lecturers-email-students-goes-viral-why-i-am-not),

November 21, 2013.

Cox, Harvey. "The Market as God," essay published in *The Atlantic Monthly,* March 1999, reprinted in *The Best Christian Writing 2000,* John Wilson, editor, (HarperSanFrancisco, 2000), p. 80-81, 91.

Chrysostom, St. John. Quoted in *Doing Well and Doing Good,* by Os Guinness, (NavPress, 2001), p. 38, 50, 56.

Daly, Hermann (and John Cobb). *For the Common Good,* (Beacon Press, 1994), page 138.

Diamond, Larry and Mosbacher, Jack. "Petroleum to the People: Africa's Coming Resource Curse—and How to Avoid It," *Foreign Affairs,* September/October 2013, p. 86-87.

Dyson, Freeman. *Disturbing the Universe,* (Harper & Row, 1979), p. 250.

Eliot, T.S. *Christianity and Culture*, (Harcourt, 1976), first published 1939, p. 17-18.

Ellul, Jacques. *To Will and To Do,* (Pilgrim Press, 1969), p. 107–108.

Gates, Jeff. *The Ownership Solution,* (Addison-Wesley, 1998), p. xxi, 4, 9, 31, 33, 62, 219, 223.

Gilder, George. *Wealth and Poverty,* (ICS Press, 1993), p. 57, 69, 79, 275.

Gilder, George. *Essay entitled Soul of Silicon,* p. 2, 9.

Glynn, Patrick. *God: The Evidence: The Reconciliation of Faith and Reason in a Post-Secular World* (Prima Publishing, 1999), p. 22, 25

Godin, Seth. *Permission Marketing,* (Simon & Schuster, 1999), p. 42.

Goolsbee, Austan. "The Volker Way: Lessons from the Last Great Hero of Modern Finance," *Foreign Affairs,* January/February 2013, p. 170.

Goudzwaard, Bob. *Idols of Our Time,* (InterVarsity Press, 1984), p. 13, 21.

Guinness, Os. *Dining with the Devil, (*Baker, 1993), p. 86.

Guinness, Os. *The Call,* (Word, 1998), p. 85, 93–94, 112, 131, 135–136.

Guinness, Os. *The Journey: Our Quest for Faith and Meaning,* (NavPress, 2001), p. 154)

Guinness, Os. Quoting a Nazi prison camp doctor, *When No One Sees: The Importance of Character in the Age of Image,* (NavPress, 2000), p. 281.

Gurteen, Stephen Humphreys. Quoted in *Doing Well and Doing Good: Money, Giving, and Caring in a Free Society,* by Os Guinness, (NavPress, 2001), p. 156.

Handy, Charles. *The Hungry Spirit,* (Broadway, 1998), p. 71–72.

Julian of Norwich. Quoted in *From the Library of C.S. Lewis: Selections from Writers Who Influenced His Spiritual Journey,* compiled by James Stuart Bell, (Waterbrook Press, 2004), p. 50.

Kelly, Kevin. *New Rules for the New Economy,* (Viking Press, 1998), p. 59.

Keyes, Richard. "The Idol Factory," essay published in *No God But God: Breaking with the Idols of our Age,* by Os Guinness and John Seel, editors, (Moody Press, 1992), p. 33.

Keynes, John Maynard. "Economic Possibilities for Our Grandchildren" in *Essays in Persuasion,* p. 369.

Kiyosaki, Robert. *Rich Dad, Poor Dad,* (TechPress Inc., 1999), p. 50, 51, 59.

Lewis, C.S. *Mere Christianity,* (HarperCollins, 2001), first published 1952, p. 56, 226-227.

Lewis, C.S. *The Weight of Glory,* (HarperCollins, 2001), first published in 1949, p. 26, 31.

Malone, Michael S. *In Fast Company,* June/July 1997, p. 102.

Mangalwadi, Vishal. *The Book That Made Your World: How the Bible Created the Soul of Western Civilization,* (Thomas Nelson, 2011), p. 70, 134, 300.

McGurn, William. "Pulpit Economics," in *First Things,* (April 2002), p. 22.

Meeks, M. Douglas. *God the Economist: The Doctrine of God and Political Economy,* (Fortress Press, 1989).

Monsma, George. Quoted in *On Moral Business* by Max Stackhouse, (Eerdmans, 1995), p. 37.

Mott, Stephen Charles. Quoted in *On Moral Business,* p. 72–74.

Muller, Jerry Z. "Capitalism and Inequality: What the Right and the Left Get Wrong", *Foreign Affairs,* March/April 2013, p. 44.

Novak, Michael. Quoted in *On Moral Business,* p. 906.

Novak, Michael. *The Spirit of Democratic Capitalism,* (Madison Books, 1991), p. 346, 356.

Petersen, Jim, Glenn McMahan, and David Russ. *More Than Me,* (NavPress, 2008), p. 35, 93.

Peterson, Eugene. *The Message,* (NavPress, 1995).

Phillips, J.B. *New Testament Christianity,* (Hodder & Stoughton, 1956), p. 115.

Pope John Paul II. *Centesimus Annus, Encyclical on the Social Order,* (Pauline Books & Media, 1991), p. 62.

Pope John Paul II. Quoted in *On Moral Business,* p. 494.

Postman, Neil. *Technopoly,* (Vintage Books, 1993), p. 54.

Reich, Robert. *The Future of Success: Working and Living in the New Economy,* (Vintage Books, 2002), p. 5, 195-196.

Sapori, Armando. *The Italian Merchant in the Middle Ages,* (Norton, 1970), p. 23.

Schaeffer, Francis A. *How Should We Then Live?,* (Fleming Revell, 1976), p. 227.

Schlossberg, Herb. *Idols for Destruction,* (Thomas Nelson, 1983), p. 11, 92, 107-108, 118, 130-131, 281, 313.

Schluter, Michael. *Beyond Capitalism: Towards a Relational Economy,* (Jubilee Center, Vol. 19, No. 1, March 2010), p.2.

Schmookler, Andrew Bard. *The Illusion of Choice,* (SUNY Press, 1993), p. 34, 99.

Sennett, Richard. *The Corrosion of Character,* (Norton & Company, 1998), p. 24–25, 26, 148.

Sider, Ronald J. *Rich Christians in an Age of Hunger,* (Word, 1997), p. 81.

Solzhenitsyn, Aleksandr. Essay entitled "At Century's End," Alti Publishing, 1995, pages 7, 9, 13, 15.

Sproul Jr., R.C. *Money Matters,* (Tyndale, 1985), p. 34–35, 102.

Stanley & Danko. *The Millionaire Next Door,* (Longstreet Press, 1996), p. 11–12.

Stark, Rodney. *The Rise of Christianity,* (Princeton University Press, 1996), p. 82,

208, 201, 212.

Stark, Rodney. The Victory of Reason, (Random House, 2005), p. 38, 55, 62-63, 76-77, 227.

Steiner, George. Quoted in *The Call*, by Os Guinness, (Word, 1998), p. 119.

Storkey, Alan. "Postmodernism Is Consumption," Chapter 6 from *Christ and Consumerism: Critical Reflections on the Spirit of Our Age*, by Thorsten Moritz and Craig Bartholomew, (Paternoster, 2000).

Tozer, A.W. *The Pursuit of God*, (Christian Publications, 1958), p. 21.

Tinder, Glenn. *Against Fate*, p. 17, 80-81.

Tinder, Glenn. *Liberty: Rethinking an Imperiled Ideal*, (Eerdmans, 2007), p. 19, 42.

Veblen, Thorstein. *The Theory of the Leisure Class*, 1899.

Volf, Miroslav. *Exclusion and Embrace: A Theological Exploration of Identity, Otherness, and Reconciliation*, (Abingdon Press, 1996), p. 131.

Wilberforce, William. Quoted in *Entrepreneurs of Life: Faith and the Venture of Purposeful Living*, by Os Guinness, NavPress, 2001), p. 214.

Wilson, Rodney. *Economics, Ethics and Religion*, (New York University Press, 1997), p. 97, 99.

Woods, Thomas E. Jr. *How the Catholic Church Built Western Civilization*, p. 176, 203.

World Bank, The. PovertyNet website, definition of Social Capital.

Wright, N.T. *The Challenge of Jesus*, (InterVarsity Press, 1999), p. 180.

Wright, Christopher. *God's People in God's Land*, (Eerdmans, 1990), p. 112.

Wuthnow, Robert. *Poor Richard's Principle*, (Princeton University Press, 1996), page 304.

Made in the USA
Charleston, SC
28 August 2016